Now L.

A tale of

This book is a testament to Daksha Trivedi's brave journey through an aggressive cancer which brings to light the power of hope as she learns to accept uncertainty. Her road less travelled takes us through an unexpected diagnosis, the challenges of treatment decisions and recovery from a life- threatening surgery. Her deeply moving story, whilst that of survival embraces the reality of her condition and conveys profound themes of relentless determination and a commitment to positive strategies at a time of pain and suffering. She discovers the true meaning of faith, love and courage that overcomes all fears. In her honest and inspiring account, she shares her learnings to live a life full of gratitude and purpose.

This book was completed during the Coronavirus (Covid-19) pandemic and subesequent lock down changing our lives forever. 'Now Living the Dream' brings a beacon of hope at a time when we are facing the greatest of uncertainties.

As an academic researcher and an epidemiologist, her work aims to provide access to evidence-based health care for patient benefit. She has witnessed many cancer patients going through their individual journeys and acknowledges the dearth of evidence on what works to improve patient outcomes in many cancers particularly gastrointestinal cancers. Complimentary and holistic approaches have a significant supportive role in patient well-being. Daksha explores the use of various tools that do enhance well-being, quality of life and recovery, with a view that our physical, mental, emotional and spiritual aspects of health are interconnected.

All that she believed in was challenged on 28 December 2017, when Daksha was given a shocking diagnosis of an aggressive cancer in lower oesophagus, soon after her twin brother passed away with a similar primary diagnosis which had advanced to his stomach and was inoperable. Daksha, together with her husband and her aging mother, charted the course of her illness, treatment and recovery with great courage and hope overcoming all fears including the fear of death. This poignant and human tale of surviving cancer is blended with the flavor of light- hearted humour. 'Now living the dream' draws together everything Daksha and her family have learnt about living well in the moment being grateful for the gift of time.

"These noble souls almost spent, having journeyed through the tunnel of aloneness and uncertainty; through valleys of despair and confusion: they overcome the corrosive acidity of fear and other challenges too numerous to mention. Eventually they get over the wall, returning to their communities with messages of hope, passing on the baton called inspiration to all of us within our unique situations. Such a one is Daksha Trivedi. Regardless of our individual profile, Daksha's chronicles of her journey "Now living the Dream" is her gift to us. She is truly a champion of hope."

-*George Harris, Renowned British actor in Theatre, TV & Radio, featuring in great films including Raiders of the Lost Ark, Frankeinstein, Harry Potter. George is an inspiration to many, both on and off screen, even when faced with extreme health issues. His smile and determination in pursuit of harmony encourages others to be champions of hope.*

Now
Living the
Dream

A tale of surviving cancer

"There is no greater agony than bearing an untold story inside you"

– Zora Neale Hurston

First published by Dr Daksha Trivedi 2020

Book cover and other designs - by Jill Bransby

The quotes used in this book are relevant to the essence of my personal journey. Although every judicious effort has been made to authenticate the source and/or author, in some cases, it was not possible to ascertain the origin. In the case of uncertainty, I have attributed it as unknown. I have selected the version that seemed most appropriate to the narrative. Where possible, permissions have been granted from the appropriate authorities and individuals for the use of quotes/poems/figures.

ISBN: 978-1-911412-91-5

Published by Dolman Scott Ltd
www.dolmanscott.co.uk

Acknowledges

The intention of the author is to offer information of a general nature which may help you. She does not prescribe the use of any particular approach to improve well-being without medical or a qualified practitioner's advice.

The author intends to donate proceeds from the sale of this book to appropriate charities.

Namaste
(nah-mahs-tay)
My soul honours your soul
I honour the place in you where
the entire universe resides.
I honour the light, love, truth,
beauty and peace within you,
because it is also within me.
In sharing these things
we are united, we are the same,
we are one.

Dedication

This book is dedicated to all those who gave me hope and courage during my darkest hours.

To my great mother whose love, boundless faith and prayers carried me through the storms into the safe harbour of life.

To my beloved husband whose love, strength and confidence sustained us through our most difficult times. I am deeply grateful for his insightful contribution in making this book possible.

Above all, to my spiritual master Sri Sathya Sai Baba whose Divine inspiration helped me to walk this arduous journey with faith, trust and forbearance. To Him I am eternally grateful for this second chance of life.

Acknowledgements

I have been very fortunate to have wonderful people around me whose love has encouraged me to write this book. A special note of thanks goes to a few friends for their help and contribution. Judith Berry, Sheila Leavy and Sue Chapman for their valuable feedback, constructive suggestions and patient proof reading on the final draft; Jill Bransby for her intuitive and artistic sketches that brought my story to life.

I am grateful to Macmillan Cancer Support and the members of the Mid Bedfordshire Cancer Support Group whose shared experiences have made a meaningful contribution. A special mention to the team at 'Together Against Cancer', Leicester for allowing me to conduct a healing workshop and share my story for encouraging others. My special thanks to Dr K Narasimhan (Director, Sri Sathya Sai Mobile Hospital SSSMH, Puttaparthi, South India), Dr D K V Prasad (Surgical Gastroenterologist, Lucknow and SSSMH) and Dr Rashmi Mehta (UK) for their insightful direction and encouraging advice.

A thankful appreciation to the Cross-Cancer Institute, Edmonton, Alberta, Canada for granting me the permission to use 'Tiles' created by patients, families, volunteers and health care professionals.

My heartfelt gratitude to my General Practitioner, Dr Helen Collins and to the dedicated medical teams at Lister Hospital, Stevenage and the Watford General Hospital, in particular, Mr Ahmed Al- Bahrani, (lead clinician of the Upper Gastrointestinal Cancer Centre for Hertfordshire and South Bedfordshire) for their timely intervention without which this book would not be a message of hope.

Important others

There are no words to express my gratitude to all those countless well- wishers who lifted me during my recovery through their visits, positive thoughts and healing prayers. My personal thanks to my colleagues from the University of Hertfordshire and Hughes Hall, University of Cambridge for their good wishes. Also included are our dear friends from many faiths and beliefs and from the various centres of Sathya Sai International Organisation (Hatfield, Luton, London, Coventry, Milton Keynes, Bangalore, South India, New York), friends from the Christian world, the North Hertfordshire Interfaith forum, Welwyn Hatfield Interfaith Group and to all noteworthy families and friends, too many to name here. I will forever be indebted to them for their love and kindness.

My thanks to Paul and Sharon Hudson for bringing Badger, the delightful Alaskan Malamute, whenever I needed him the most.

In praise of

Now Living the Dream

A tale of surviving cancer

"This book has been written by Daksha at a pivotal time in her life, a diagnosis of oesophageal cancer and a recovery journey that is both moving and one that other cancer patients can relate to. Daksha provides the narrative, the story, that is often unseen or not voiced in the cancer literature. She describes in depth the impact of diagnosis, treatment and her approach to recovery in a way that someone who is also on that journey, like me, can feel. The thoughts and feelings that it invokes – fear of death, of pain and the effects of treatment, anger, why me, but also the vital comfort, compassion and support of others and the profound importance of love and faith in the survival journey. Recovery becomes the here and now of being alive, celebrating life, the dream that as a cancer patient we long to realise and share with those we love. As a nurse as well as a patient, I have experienced cancer from both sides now and I truly believe that health care professionals would find this book uplifting and helpful in their day to day work with all cancer patients, regardless of age or diagnosis. The insights are a remarkable testimony to Daksha's own survival and provide hope and belief for those of us who are still on our own journey."

- *Professor Sally Kendall, MBE, PhD, RN, RHV, FQNI, MFPH*
  Recovering from breast cancer.

"Receiving a major medical diagnosis is a significant life-turning event for all of us, a crucial time of decision making, particularly as to what mental and spiritual course we will pursue going forward. Many cancer survivors say that their diagnosis was ultimately one of the most positive experiences in their lives because it served as the impetus for them to reshape their way of being in the world. In this inspiring story, Dr Daksha Trivedi shares with us just that decision in her own life, to activate and deeply embrace her inner spiritual essence and the healing power of her mind. With these resources as her foundation, she pursued a combination of conventional and holistic approaches to reclaim her health and to foster a life of greater wellbeing. Dr Trivedi now spreads this guiding message of hope, empowerment, and transformation to others."

- *Paul J. Mills, PhD; Professor and Chief at the University of California San Diego's (UCSD) Department of Family Medicine and Public Health, Director of the UCSD Center of Excellence for Research and Training in Integrative Health, Director of the UCSD Clinical Research Biomarker Laboratory, Director of research for the Deepak Chopra Foundation.*

"Dr. Trivedi was given the shocking diagnosis of aggressive oesophageal cancer. We experience the monumental challenges of an awful diagnosis, the gut-wrenching treatment and long recovery through her eyes. She poignantly relays her journey with a no-holds-bar honesty and vulnerability that leaves you speechless. Daksha audaciously shares her innermost thoughts, insecurities and fears and channels these to cultivate wisdom, compassion and courage with surprising serenity. When the life she knew comes to a halt and her reality suspended - she embraces the emptiness and openness imputed of meaning and lives for the NOW. Her disease serves as a catalyst for her spiritual metamorphosis, a seed for her awakening."

- *Falguni Bhatt, Social care, policy and planning, University of Columbia, Masters in Social Work, Maharaja Sayajirao University, India. Licensed Certified Social Worker, Counsellor and Psychotherapist, University of State of New York; Reiki Practitioner*

"A remarkable, deeply moving and inspiring account of Dr Trivedi's cancer journey. When faced with a life- threatening diagnosis, Daksha found the strength to rise above the shock, fear and uncertainty, which always accompanies a serious cancer diagnosis. She eloquently details her story from diagnosis, through surgery and its unpleasant aftereffects, to rebuilding her life with renewed vigour. Lovingly supported by her husband and mum - this is an inspirational book which will resonate with every cancer patient. Together Against Cancer supports people at any stage of cancer journey, 'Now Living the Dream' will definitely be in our library."

- *Stephen Gamble, Education and Wellness Manager, Together Against Cancer, UK; Naturopathic nutritionist PDNN; Gerson Therapy Practitioner (Gerson Institute, UK)*

"In "Now Living the Dream" Dr Trivedi has provided us with a riveting account of her physical cancer journey. We follow her progress, and those of her estimable husband and mother, through an emotional roller-coaster of clinical appointments and procedures. However, into this narrative she has woven most moving insights into her spiritual journey, informed as it is by her own cultural and spiritual background. This well-written and highly accessible book is an indispensable read for anyone (or their friends and relatives) who is on their own cancer journey and is above all a great testimony to the power of faith. She truly is a remarkable lady!"

- *Eddie Thompson, BA LLB; Retired paralegal and teacher; Fellow Oesophageal cancer patient*

"From a world of academia, Daksha was plunged into a tumultuous cancer journey two years ago. I have known her since childhood in Kenya, always eager, self-motivated and determined, excelling in everything she did. I am therefore not surprised that she became a brave warrior against the barrage of challenges including a totally life changing surgical intervention. In her book, the author eloquently depicts her strength, self- belief, love for life, deep faith, and unconditional love and support from her husband and her dear mother.

As a general practitioner, I find that Daksha's convincing experience supports the notion that those who believe in the body's innate ability to heal can often have a better outcome. She blends science, medicine and spirituality and offers practical strategies that helped her. I encourage everyone to read this powerfully inspiring book for we never know where our paths will take us. Thank you, Dr Trivedi for sharing your soul stirring journey with us."

- *Dr Rashmi Mehta, MBBS, MRCS, LRCP, special interest in holistic health and functional medicine*

"Now Living the Dream" is a classic example of the manifestation of the power of love, the living force within us which heals. It has a purpose, a dream and fulfilment even more so when illnesses are so prevalent, especially at this time of unpredictable effects of the pandemic which the whole world is facing today. Through faith, belief, hope, courage and determination, Daksha has proved that no matter how far your condition has advanced, if you choose or desire to restore your health into wellness, you actually give birth to a new desire and that is when " the power of wellness emerges". A must read not only for cancer patients but for every human being who walks on the face of the Earth."

- *Lim Cheng Hoe, Former International Badminton Coach to Sweden, Iceland and Zambia; former representative of the Malaysian Badminton Team; Retired Teacher and Trustee for mainstream Education, UK; Currently an International Reiki Master, Trainer & Tai-Chi Practitioner, UK*

"This is a brave book about an inner and outer journey after being diagnosed with cancer of the oesophagus. The physical implications of this diagnosis and subsequent surgery and treatment were devastating, but what is so compelling about this testament is the author's willingness to share how she reflected on and rigorously examined the daily challenges which threatened her existence. Life as experienced before surgery would never be the same again but the new life, which continues to unfold, is one with rich spiritual meaning, tremendous gratitude for each moment and deep compassion for all beings. This book is a great inspiration and encouragement for all who wish to live life fully with joy, healing and appreciation of the present moment."

>   -   *Judith Berry, Retired Primary School Headteacher, T.C. Alexander Teachers' College Sydney Australia; Member of the Findhorn Foundation Community Scotland; Actively involved in the Care Sector of the Community and Conservation Charities.*

"As a Barrister and a Professor of Law, I rarely find myself struggling to find the right words to pen or to say. This, however, is one such occasion. Having known Dr Trivedi not only through her dedicated work in promoting health and wellbeing including the activities of Sathya Sai International Organisation, UK, but also personally, I was somewhat shocked to learn of her 'health' condition as conveyed to me by her husband. Based on my spiritual beliefs, I was inspired to pray for her or as one would say send her 'mantra induced vibrational energy'. What Daksha has accomplished through this book is nothing short of offering solace and hope for the multitude who are in a similar position by recounting her trials and tribulations as well as her experiences. The wonderful and sincere accounts speak volumes of her, and I can only say that even in this state, she is living the expression: 'Service to Man is Service to God'. I hope that all who read 'Now Living the Dream' will learn to empower themselves when faced with dilemmas just as Daksha has conveyed in her courageous journey of survival."

- *Dr Vickneswaren Krishnan, Barrister (Middle Temple)*
  & Visiting Professor of International Law (Botswana),
  Hindu Chaplain, University of Cambridge

"Dr Daksha Trivedi writes a passionate and meticulous description of her personal journey with cancer. She has captured the role of body, mind, spirit and emotions that play an integral part in recovery and healing. Daksha has acknowledged and honored spirituality, culture, family, friends and health care providers as key elements to her victory over cancer. Her acceptance of the diagnosis, treatment and support helps her to survive cancer and results in "Now Living the Dream", a great message that inspires us all. "

- *Dr Ranee Thayala Richards, MBBS, MPM, FRANZCP;*
  Consultant Psychiatrist, Dandenong Hospital, Monash
  Health, Victoria, Australia

"As someone who went through the same Oesophageal cancer as Daksha did, albeit eleven years ago, I found this to be an inspirational story. The way that she and her family went through the ordeal supported by each other's love and unwavering faith will be a source of hope and inspiration to all who read this book."

- *Dave Simpson, former Oesophageal cancer patient*

"Sometimes we cannot see the light at the end of the tunnel, this is because there are always twists and turns in life. Daksha's book teaches us to keep walking and eventually despite the many deviations we must not give up, and we will see the light again. This book will be useful to support people who have cancer and are beginning that journey, down that long tunnel. She covers the shock of diagnosis, the fear, the hope of recovery, the many trials and tribulations, and eventual cure. She clearly describes her journey providing numerous ideas that people will find helpful in overcoming their own anxieties and fears. She provides practical advice and a touching honesty about her own experiences. Reading it was a privilege.

- *Professor Mike Kirby, MBBS, LRCP, MRCS, FRCP; Clinician & Academic; Prostate Cancer Charity Research Advisory Group, The Prostate Centre, London. Member of UK Department of Health Prostate Cancer Risk Management Working Party & several National Health Service advisory boards.*

"Daksha is an epidemiologist and a scientist; a woman of great faith who is supported by family and friends who share faiths; and someone who is able to tell the story of her journey through oesophageal cancer from beginning to recovery, sparing no detail and with no emotional holds barred. This book is her story interwoven with interesting science and discussions of aspects of faith and emotional support (helping those of 'no faith' to appreciate positive mindset and self- empowerment); accompanied by quotations from classical and modern literature and personal photographs; but also containing much practical advice. We all think we know what 'holistic care' means, but most do not fully understand what it is unless we have experienced it or read this book."

-   *Dr Paul Siklos, MA (Cantab), BSc, MBBS, FRCP; Consultant Physician (retired), West Suffolk Hospital, NHS Foundation Trust, UK; Associate Clinical Dean (retired), University of Cambridge School of Clinical Medicine; Life Fellow, Hughes Hall, Cambridge; Winner of the Pilkington Prize 2005 award in recognition of teaching excellence.*

"Dr Daksha Trivedi has written a profoundly inspiring account of her unforeseen but an aggressive cancer diagnosis. She narrates openly her vulnerability laced with deep anxieties, emotions, trials and tribulations in the face of great uncertainty. The disease is one which requires a number of diagnostic modalities, some of them done repeatedly. She went through all of them with grit and determination, factors which greatly help the treating doctors and aid the healing process. Throughout her treatment journey,

I monitored her closely and her understanding of the problem, which she was able to face with courage and determination. Her book gifts us with practical ways to overcome adversity and to embrace such a journey with courage and faith. A professional and a patient, Daksha speaks of hope, love and gratitude, reminding us of what really matters in life. She delicately brings together science, medicine and spirituality, understanding the difficulties. Dr Trivedi brings remarkable insight and wisdom which will no doubt touch the hearts of many. It is my wish that every medical professional and every patient going through this journey reads the book and I am sure it will help them greatly surmount the steep challenges. This book deserves a wide circulation for all."

- *Dr K Narasimhan, MBBS, MNAMS (Medicine) Director of Sri Sathya Sai (SSS) Mobile Hospital, Medical Superintendent of SSS General Hospital, Puttaparthi, South India; Winner of the CNBC-TV 18 Healthcare Award, India*

Contents

Contents

Foreword

In writing a foreword for this book about a cancer journey, I wondered how I would word it. Three simple words "You have cancer" finds the darkest place in your heart and hits those loved ones around you. In a moment, your life is thrown into a huge chasm staring into the void.

In reading this tale of surviving cancer, I looked back and could relate to my own oesophageal cancer journey. Daksha's powerful narrative reflects this in a way that is as personal as can be but is also true for **all** cancer patients to relate to their journey. Her journey echoes the emotions, the fears and the knowledge of how fragile life is, sadly for many, the diagnosis is too late. This transformative story gives hope and happiness we wish on everyone with cancer and their families who silently suffer along the way.

Daksha's cancer pathway shows how important those around us all are, our loved ones and friends to support us, our many varied beliefs of someone watching over us, the fantastic National Health Service (NHS UK) with the skills of treatment and compassion and the medical researchers who give us the hope and life we all deserve. In addition, Daksha shares some of her helpful strategies for overcoming both physical and emotional difficulties discovering what truly matters in life. Though she charts her deeply personal experience, the book has a universal reach through her perspective both as a patient and an academic.

My pathway from diagnosis has taken me on a road of discovery into patient support, research for patients to understand the many trials they are invited to join and to Chairing the Oesophageal Patients Association (OPA), all things totally alien to my world of printing! The OPA was founded some 35 years ago as a charity by David Kirby, OBE to support Oesophageal cancer patients. His meritorious effort in promoting patient to patient support was the key in helping patients living beyond cancer. It is encouraging to read that Daksha has addressed the need to support cancer patients and their families, particularly those living in rural areas.

Cancer will not go away but we can reduce the toll on life by awareness, early diagnosis, research, treatment and support right from the start to patients by patients, not forgetting that belief in hope is a big part of the healing.

This remarkable book is a testament to Dr Trivedi's tremendous courage and faith as she unravels the complexities of this triumphant human journey.

By David Chuter, Chairman OPA; supported by David Kirby, OBE; Founder & Life President, OPA

David Chuter, Chairperson, Guildford Surrey UK Support Group; Representative on The National Institute for Health and Care Excellence (NICE), contributing to NICE guidance for improving health and social care; Patient Ambassador: National Cancer Research Institute Consumer Liaison Group; World Cancer Research Fund; Cancer Research UK; Governor, NHS Royal Surrey Hospital

Foundation Trust; Advisor to patient support groups across Europe for gastrointestinal cancers.

Introduction

The greatest gift

God gave us the gift of life; it is up to us to give ourselves the gift of living well

- Voltaire

My heart sank upon hearing three words "You have cancer". Every day in the UK, around one thousand people hear these frightening words, and I never envisaged that I would be one of them. Life as we know it can vanish in a heartbeat and the unthinkable can happen in a moment. My twin brother whose face I remember so vividly, drained of hope and with pleading tearful eyes had uttered "please pray for me". It was like his spirit was stolen from an unseen injury. I cried a river for my beloved brother's plight. Sadly, he died of advanced stomach cancer within the year given to him. It beggars belief that only after six months I could face the same predicament. The shock and disbelief were hard to bear, and the overwhelming numbness incapacitated my family. We were gripped into a spiral of recurring thoughts about cancer and its unpredictable outcome.

In my altered state, I assumed the worst which exploded my fears and emotions throwing me into the abyss. "Am I dying?" "Has it spread?" were the words that re-opened the wounds before they had time to heal. The effects of this uninvited growth within my body, would soon spread to my family, friends and my professional life. For almost three months I suffered deeply in silence from the uncertainty of the treatment plan, during which time I wish I could have found the necessary support from those who had undergone a similar experience. The most frightening aspect was not knowing whether the treatment would work and what would happen to me. Whilst the medical professionals have a reasonable idea about how many people will benefit from a particular type of treatment, they can never be certain how individuals will respond.

As an epidemiologist, I can say with certainty that the probability of dying is still one hundred percent. Until we have a close encounter with a life-threatening condition, we refuse to accept the possibility of our own demise. Paradoxically, many faiths teach us to accept life and death with equanimity to minimise our suffering. Therefore, our potential to be fully human and fully alive does not necessarily depend on the presence or absence of cancer. Receiving this unexpected news radically changed all my preconceptions of how my life should be.

Having spent many years researching various chronic diseases, it dawned on me that fear remains the most chronic disease of our generation and finding a cure for it becomes paramount. My doctoral work had examined new ways of diagnosing breast cancer so that treatment could be targeted for cancer specific tumour markers. Working with Professors Harold Baum, the singing biochemist and Professor Michael Baum, a specialist in breast cancer treatment, I learnt to apply intelligent determination. I observed patients coming through the clinic, many expressing powerful emotions, namely denial, anger and guilt, preparing for death, whilst those who transcended these, had somehow conquered their fear of death. Only when I became a patient, I understood that there is no good cancer or bad cancer, there is just cancer with a big C. However hard we try, it is almost impossible to escape the word, which is like a dark menacing and a devouring shadow. Standing at the crossroads of life and death, this perfect storm which came from nowhere demanded a shift in my thinking about mortality. It was not about a new lease of life but more about viewing life differently.

Memories from my past welled up intense emotions raising fundamental questions. How did I get here? My life until now had to be perfect without question where academic excellence was the expected norm. I have lived with fear of failure, sickness and death, but mostly the fear of being alone. The familiar faces of my family had faded over time into the "matchstick men" as portrayed in L.S. Lowry's painting. Even though my family life was somewhat fragmented, I pursued relentlessly the exciting field of science and medicine. I knew there had to be more to this world and my place in it than my limited understanding would allow. The great and the good have asked the same questions - Who am I, why am I here and what is the purpose of my life? My path of self-enquiry to this point has favoured me with valuable insights, but now my past juxtaposed with a crushing diagnosis. This insolitus occurrence became the catalyst for me to reflect on my life trying to make sense of what was happening to me.

Seeking answers to life's questions, I had embarked on a personal odyssey for so long to discover a meaning to my existence. Many pilgrimages took me to India, the mystical land of my forefathers, full of scholarly knowledge and culturally exotic. I had a numinous experience at various places of worship and in contemplative silence,

I learnt the wisdom from the holy scriptures and their exposition from the revered sages, hoping to change the quality of my life and find contentment.

Over three decades ago, upon closing the last page of James Hilton's book "The Lost Horizon", my destiny took me to Prasanthi Nilayam (Abode of Supreme Peace) in Puttaparthi, a remote village in South India. There, I discovered my Shangri-La amidst an ocean of humanity - people from different faiths, traditions or no faith, all desperately seeking something known only to them. My first encounter with Sathya Sai Baba had a profound and a lasting effect on me. I experienced an unfamiliar serenity in which questions close to my heart emerged. The aesthetic touch of the Divine shrouded me in a vibrational field of radiant energy, which I now recognise as love in its purest form. The essence that exists in us, but often remains buried under layers of pain, suffering and turbulent relationships. The seeds of faith and self-enquiry had been planted and I knew I was on the right path of self-realisation. This was my Rosetta Stone moment helping me to decipher the code of my life. It symbolised a greater consciousness of strength and energy, where man and God become one.

My calling to Lourdes surrounded by blue mountains was another defining experience in my journey of self-discovery. Through eons of time, man has seen spectacular sunrises over the mighty rivers that flow with an ineffable power. As I stood by the Gave de Pau, the notion of time dissolved and I was in a unique place called 'now'. Here, neither my past nor my future had any significance and this special moment was given to me for cleansing my soul.

Along my life's journey, I had the privilege to work with eminent academics, scientists, doctors, spiritual thinkers and healing practitioners who helped me to interpret the complex tapestry of life. Now faced with a crisis, I was able to draw upon those valuable insights that became a bedrock upon which my life would unfold.

As a Reiki practitioner, I recall my first visit a few years ago to "Together against Cancer" (TAC) in Leicester, where I met many people at different stages of their cancer journey. I was amazed by their sense of what really mattered to them, their changed priorities and how much they embraced life, despite their daily struggle with their illness. During our sessions and conversations, I discovered that many had overcome their fear of dying and had learnt the art of living well. This was something beyond the usual regime of medical treatment. I was able to steer them into developing mindfulness, a positive mind-set and self- empowerment to aid healing and recovery. Their tenacity to try and overcome their hardships greatly inspired me and little did I anticipate that one day I would be walking the same path. Many people take the view that not talking about it or being in denial is their best method of coping with the crisis. Some people do cope better by not talking about cancer. However I learnt that this approach can also be damaging to such an extent that people are unable to make rational decisions about their treatment.

My scientific training had convinced me that there was nothing beyond statistics and analysis, but I soon learnt that research reports on probabilities, largely based on population data and individuals do not necessarily fit into these probabilities. For example, people who smoke are likely to get lung cancer, but not all lung cancer patients have been smokers. I had come across people who were given 'a few months to live' surprisingly outlive their given prognosis, whereas others with more encouraging prospects unexpectedly deteriorated. Science lends itself to analytical frameworks, but can these really encompass life, death, prognosis and recovery? Every cell in our body has an inborn intelligence to heal and our body can support this in every way. When this process is accepted in our consciousness, physical healing can take place. Each moment then marks a new beginning. We do not fully understand all the factors that have contributed to the development of cancer, so instead of focusing on looking for reasons, it would be better for us to pay attention to our own needs, learning to look after ourselves and get the support we desperately need.

This book is a humble offering to you, and I hope it will help you to accept painful uncertainties and rise above them. In doing so, we can conquer fear as we never really know when death comes knocking at our door. Along the way, I have received the comforting hand of a stranger during my most painful moments which has made a huge difference. The intricacies of human condition, often hanging by the thread between life and death remind us that we can find meaning even for a short while for our existence. Cancer comes as a memento mori, reminding us that we will die. We are then in a spectrum between submissive acceptance to a total denial. In time, we wake up to the reality we face when Pegasus breathes new life in us. If we are mindful of this inevitable fate, our lives would be entirely different.

I hope that my testimony will empower you to live every moment knowing that how we think affects us at every level. I have lived *in* fear, *through* fear and finally learnt to *conquer* fear. When we are not afraid of death, we are no longer afraid of life and we allow ourselves to be loved unconditionally. Great saints and sages from time immemorial give us the wisdom to transcend the problem of pain by going beyond ourselves and our body consciousness. Separating myself from this unbearable mental and physical pain prepared me for the process of self-healing. As we become free from the chains that bind us, we learn to love ourselves and to know that everything that surrounds us is love personified. We then begin to fulfil our dreams, even from the edge of life.

Many people may not have affinity to any particular faith or the existence of a supreme being, but somehow they discover an intrinsic strength which seems to carry them through their difficulties. It is not only my dream, but also my wish that every patient and their family who are burdened with such a catastrophic event have access to compassionate support from the outset. Let us together treasure our greatest gift of living well whatever the adversity. It is up to us to either dread the darkness or light a little lantern of hope.

"Who am I to say 'believe' 'have faith" in the face of life's realities? I want to give you something more permanent, but I can only point the way. I have no formula for winning the race. Everyone runs in her own way or his way. And where does the power come from to see the race to its end? From Within." (Eric Liddell, from Chariots of Fire[1])

---

[1] Courtesy: Lord Puttnam's office

ONE

Life will never be the same

*Out of suffering have emerged the
strongest souls*

- Kahlil Gibran

Christmas season was upon us and we could see from our window a brightly decorated vehicle carrying a portly Santa wearing gold rimmed spectacles and a copious beard that matched a glistening silver head of hair. His eager eyes were scanning our neighbourhood, while children ran to our front door singing carols bringing a festive magic to every home. The good cheer brought us much needed hope, peace and good will, after the recent losses of our loved ones. My dear mother was looking forward to new beginnings, that would ease the unbearable pain of the past year. We so enjoy those walks in Meppershall, our beautiful village in Bedfordshire, also known as 'God's country". This time of the year was pristine with scattered snowflakes in the open countryside. The high street was adorned with multicoloured Christmas lights and the smell of fresh bread inviting us to peer inside Roger's bakery well known for its homemade cakes and mince pies. My 'pocket mum', lovingly described by my friends due to her petite frame, would hold on to me tightly as we walked, leaving a trail of tiny footprints in the soft snow.

The frosty morning of the 28th December 2017, a date we will never forget, was filled with the hustle and bustle of people preparing for the new year as we made our way to Lister Hospital in Stevenage, Hertfordshire. There is never a good day to receive bad news. My husband, Pradip, and I were ushered into the consultant's office leaving my mother waiting outside. Seeing a Macmillan nurse entering the office, my heart began to pound against my chest. We did not know where the fine balance lay - between welcoming the bearer of the news or to fear them.

Seated in front of the consultant, we heard her clinical voice "You have something complex going on in your lower oesophagus (food pipe). You have cancer." I leaned across and looked at the scans and the results on her computer screen, quickly grasping what was being conveyed. From this moment, everything felt surreal as we descended into utter shock and disbelief. Pradip's face turned white as he went into a distressed state, tears welling up in his eyes. I blurted out "I am not having you like this." I pleaded, staring at the consultant "What am I to tell an 87-year-old mother waiting outside who has already lost two sons and a husband?". There must be a mistake, I thought, given I had no symptoms suggesting such a devastating diagnosis. I lost my composure, and forgetting all my scientific training, questions poured out of me in an incoherent manner. "What did I do wrong?" She offered no words of comfort but repeated the results" Adenocarcinoma[2] of the lower oesophagus." What if it is inoperable? How long have I got? These questions penetrated my mind with such force that I was lost for words. We were told that we would hear more from the multidisciplinary team (MDT) and at that precise moment I realised that my life would never be the same. His eyes soaked in

[2] Describes a specific type of cancer

tears, Pradip asked the consultant to check the results again. No one could see the wound that stole his spirit. He refused to accept the findings and quickly bounced back with the resolve to face boldly whatever was going to happen to us.

Our life crumbling before us and still shell shocked, we left the consultant's office with the Macmillan nurse. My mother looked at me enquiringly, as we made our way to yet another office. Little did we realise that we were being taken to the Macmillan cancer information centre. The nurse could clearly see that we were emotionally in a very difficult place trying to grapple with the news just conveyed to us, but unfortunately, she was unable to provide further help as she was not an oesophageal nurse. She sympathised with our feelings but just could not discuss 'what next'. Finding my mother waiting alone in the centre surrounded by cancer leaflets, her small face full of anxiety, I agonised over how I would be able to tell her this earth-shattering news. Our world had turned completely on its head as the three of us stood alone in the debris of the diagnosis.

With overflowing tears, we tried to drink a cappuccino in the hospital café, when my mother burst out "God, I have had my fair share". We knew in our hearts the pain she felt of losing both her boys and her husband. Her voice declared a resolute 'No', although her enquiring eyes conveyed a frightening uncertainty of what she was about to hear. We had to give her a soft landing, as we ourselves were in total disbelief and were waiting for further confirmation. I informed her correctly that unusual polyps were discovered in my food pipe which needed further investigation. When we left the hospital, we were extremely distressed, bewildered and felt abandoned. Our new year's shopping continued in an uninterested manner while the words "you have cancer" continuously played on our minds. Our drive home was disconcertingly quiet as thoughts of my twin brother's journey haunted me. Having grown up together in the same family, our paths had diverged over time, only to be reunited through his fateful diagnosis. I vaguely remembered his unusual demeanour and eating patterns which now made sense. Little did we know that this would be the last face to face contact he would have with our mother when he visited us on her 85th birthday. We wished him well and he returned back to his world in Canada. Never in my wildest dreams, did I ever foresee this would happen to me and at this moment, I had the will to say, "This is not how the story is going to end". Deepak, my twin, while bravely positive, masked his innermost concerns fearing the inevitable. In this crisis, he yearned for my help hoping that his dire situation would improve. He believed my faith would go a long way to alleviate his pain, leaving me sometimes feeling inadequate in all my efforts to support him. I saw him summon courage from deep within himself to complete whatever he felt he needed to do in the time that remained.

I was now fearful of going through the same procedures as him, enduring the same pain and worrying that my fate would be the same. It dawned on me much later that somehow being at his side had prepared me to face the challenges that were yet to come. The notorious word 'cancer' not only affected my mind and body but 'spread' to all aspects of my life and that of my immediate family.

Later that afternoon in our meditation room, Pradip and I talked with a heavy heart and informed Mum that whilst there would be further investigations, doing nothing was not an option. As more tests followed and major surgery seemed likely, my mother rebelled "They can say what they want, but this does not apply to you." She was determined to will 'the problem' away. Gradually, she took charge of the whole situation through simple faith, prayer, and unyielding determination which became the elixir of her blessings. I was astonished by her strategic planning leading the war against my diagnosis, as her denial became her coping mechanism. Her petition to God was a revelation to me, as I had never been able to pray with such conviction. It seemed as if the words 'Nil Sine Numine' (nothing without Providence) were etched in her heart.

For the first time in a long time, I felt a mother's love deep in my heart and I knew I was not abandoned. "Once I have surrendered everything to God, I have no other thought" she rebuked, refusing to engage in any 'what ifs' and pursuing her belief so doggedly.

To steer us away from any dispiriting thoughts about my condition, she would cleverly engage us in those long Bollywood films with escapist story lines alive with songs and dance. We felt like we were back in the cheap two anna seats of an Indian cinema where we would lose ourselves for a while in a spectacular make-believe world. Alas, it became a panacea for each of us, silent in our own hidden and unspoken pain.

Is it chance or destiny that comes to teach us how temporary life is? Is it the force of the unknown that turns the joys of yesterday into the wrath of today? Why has all this happened to me?

In the famous work of Leo Tolstoy (War and Peace), we learn that sufferings are our misfortunes. However, being taken a prisoner by the diagnosis, I could relate to Pierre Bezhukhov's rationale that "When our lives are knocked off course we imagine everything in them is lost. It is only the start of something new and good. As long as there is life there is happiness. There is a great deal, a great deal still to come.."

TWO

Making sense of "It"

Three months earlier, I met with Dr Helen Collins my General Practitioner (GP) to discuss my irregular bowel movements and she initially referred me for a colonoscopy for irritable bowel symptoms. Suddenly, she seemed to have a 'light bulb' moment and suggested I have the 'whole lot' meaning an endoscopy as well. As I had no other major symptoms (such as acidity, reflux, heart burn, regurgitation), I was somewhat surprised that she referred me to a gastroenterologist to have this test. In October that year, he confirmed that the endoscopy was not necessary, given I had no obvious presenting symptoms, but persuaded me to have it as I had "earnt myself the test, but we are not expecting to find anything."

Later that evening I felt the need to speak to my dear friend Dr Rashmi Mehta, a GP in Birmingham, who confirmed that she usually refers patients for an endoscopy when there are obvious symptoms or other indications. She allayed my fears and persuaded me to take these tests for my own peace of mind. Due to pressing deadlines at work, I had to defer my earlier appointment which ironically was on 11 November 2017, armistice day, marking the cessation of all hostilities at the end of The Great War. On the day of the scheduled tests later on 14 December at the endoscopy unit, I was naturally anxious about having both procedures one after the other. The gastroenterologist informed me later that he had taken a biopsy from two small polyps in my upper gastrointestinal region and at the same time assured me that the colonoscopy looked fine, raising no concerns.

After a comforting tea and a sandwich, we drove home assuming that polyps are usually harmless and can be easily removed if necessary. A week later I received a telephone call from the nurse, offering me an appointment to discuss my results. I asked her nervously whether everything was all right, and she conveyed that she had not seen my results and an appointment was made with a consultant on the 28 December 2017. This was a demanding time for me as an academic lead on a major grant proposal commissioned by the Government's National Institute for Health Research. This project had great potential for young people with depression, with involvement of UK's leading research institutes. I was looking forward to new opportunities with anticipation and excitement.

The past year marked the beginning of annus horriblis, a time of unprecedented events full of startling surprises and cascading tragedies – major burglary at home, my brother-in-law's sudden death (Hodgkin's lymphoma revealed at post mortem) and an arduous journey with my twin brother's advanced cancer culminating in this dramatic irony of my diagnosis.

We stood before life through another humbling experience which continued to teach us the simple lessons of letting go, dissolving resentments, cultivating love, understanding and tolerance for that fragile life we all take for granted. We think we will live forever, and when someone dies it is their death, not ours.

With great trepidation, I contacted Dr Rashmi Mehta again who had urged me to have this test when I was having so many doubts. Breaking the news to her proved to be quite difficult as I presumed that she might feel a sense of responsibility for this pain. I assured her that I greatly valued her insightful thinking about taking these tests, as she continued to support me.

Our revered friend Dr Narasimhan, director of the Sathya Sai Mobile Hospital in Puttaparthi, South India, spoke the kindest words after studying my endoscopy results. "As it is lower down in the oesophagus, WE will be okay, if it is localised". My eyes welled up with tears upon hearing the word WE and I knew I was not alone. I felt that God's unseen presence somehow pervaded this cataclysmic journey. What was the purpose of this event in my life and what was I to learn from all this? Dr Narasimhan had been a great source of support to me and my mother only a few months earlier during our very difficult time when my brother was terminally ill. Moreover, he looked at the various scans and reports I sent him and discussed with me the likely pathways for him, encouraging us never to lose faith and hope regardless of his prognosis. I remember that first long email I had received from my brother which conveyed the sheer devastation of his spirit. Just as my strength petered out, Anil, with whom I also share a birthday and his wife Pradyna from Puttaparthi, South India picked me up and comforted me with many uplifting spiritual conversations which continued when I began to descend into a similar quagmire.

Rajiv Shah, a close family friend, had just returned home from a medical camp in South India, when I called him to break the news, not realising that it was the anniversary of his father's death. I sensed his shock when the awkward silence was broken by his faltering voice 'we need to meet'. At his home, the next day, we discussed more, mindful that both his parents had suffered from cancer. I felt uncertain about going ahead with our planned holiday to Madeira. "We are going" he stated emphatically, and in an instant, his positive energy reached me. As we were leaving, we embraced each other, and that moment was an epiphany which enabled me to see my predicament through a prism of new light. "We are with you in this", his words of comfort stayed with me.

 Sister Pavalam, a retired nurse, originally from Sri Lanka who had worked both in France and the UK, now a senior practitioner of vibrionic healing, received us warmly and prepared some healing remedies for me. She explained that healing aims to balance our energy flow as negative tendencies can misalign our chakras or energy centres within us making us susceptible to illnesses. Now was the time to rebalance myself and restore my health. Her warm smile, unwavering faith in God and comforting words conveyed a gentle but firm assurance that all will be well. She whispered that it was not my fault, that karma has a way of working itself out and upon hearing this, I cried my heart out.

Soon after my diagnosis, Father Tom O'Brien from Our Lady Catholic Church in Hitchin, and a friend from the North Hertfordshire Interfaith forum, greeted us with a smile. Alone with my thoughts facing my mortality, I sat in a room at the church that allowed me to unburden my growing inner fears. He understood my plight, as only a few months earlier I sat in the same room seeking his counsel about my brother's cancer journey. His soothing words calmed my emotional turmoil and with the deepest of conviction, he promised that the invisible hand of the Divine would guide us through this difficult time. As I left him, he reminded me never to ask why. The comforting words of Lord Buddha that our goal is to find the blessing in every experience no matter how bad it seems, filled me with peace.

Ultimately this journey was mine and mine alone. For me, God is universal energy, a divine spirit, a pure consciousness and a living essence in each one of us. Irrespective of each person's religious beliefs there appears to be a universal belief in the existence of a higher power. Whatever path we follow, the same divine principle teaches us the oneness of each faith. I needed to be completely open removing all barriers to receive the love that heals. In the quiet recess of my heart, I sought guidance from my spiritual master, Sai Baba to take me through this calamity. People came together from various faiths holding me in their thoughts and prayers. "What can I do?" implored my husband. "Can you make time go back?!" I retorted.

Sometimes, events can make us see things imperfectly like a mirror covered with dust. Though we see things partial and incomplete, we just have to make this journey to realise that in time, all will be revealed to us to make us whole.

THREE

Coping with uncertainty

The problem is we think we have time

We snuggled together by the fireplace, holding hands watching the television when the last chime of the Big Ben ushered in the new year with an ostentatious fireworks display. The music and merriment grew into a crescendo and as we sang the Auld Lang Syne, I opened a new book of life. Its blank pages awaited the holy scribe to declare the time that may be waiting for me. The beauty and the beast of life became obvious to me from a forced awareness that the route of my destiny was unpredictable. I remained pensive, lost in the words of T. S. Eliot *"last year's words belong to last year's language, and next year's words await another voice."* My heart hungered for my pain to be healed, my wounds to speak of wisdom, my joy to be contagious, my hope to ignite me, my faith to resurrect me, my heart to embrace love and never tire of serving those in need. Fighting a melancholy surge of sadness, we just could not talk about the cancer. Instead we found comfort watching inspirational messages from Joel Osteen's televised sermons about people who had received a cancer diagnosis but knew that this was not the end of their story, that God had a plan beyond the diagnosis. He gave living examples of people emerging victorious and becoming restored through the power of belief which enabled them to focus positively on being healed.

Walking along the high street lined with trees, I gazed at them with a new curiosity noticing that some had lost their autumn glow from vibrant colours and were turning to the brown tones complemented by a winter fragrance. The morning chorus of the birds' opera stirred my soul as if in response to my heart ache. Dogs that scared me for many years were now sniffing and playing around me, not allowing me to ignore them. I wondered if they somehow sensed something unusual within me and noticed my despair, letting me know that I was not alone? It came as no surprise to me when I later came across case reports of dogs being able to sense various cancers. Moments became precious as cancer would soon take a centre stage in our lives. I was overcome with the guilt of my diagnosis and the huge burden to come upon my family, especially my mother whose denial stemmed from the pain buried in her heart. During the time between diagnosis and treatment, I suffered the slings and arrows of this misfortune. When our village community gradually became aware of the difficult situation I was in, some chose to look the other way and walk away from me. Others came once but never to return whereas strangers smiled with kindness giving me courage which at the time I needed the most. I now understand that fear can be so elusive that people can be paralysed not knowing what to say or do when they see us or our loved ones. I believed that people could not cope as they were scared just when I wanted them to be brave for me.

In this helpless state, I dwelt constantly about enduring pain and treatment, and my ability to have a normal life, should I survive this onslaught. Learning to live in the present and discover a higher purpose through this incredible journey became my ultimate aim.

We had to discuss everything sensitively with my dear mother as the word 'cancer' would devastate her and like in many South Asian families the worst is often assumed. Therefore, it was not possible for us to discuss this openly with our nearest and dearest, being careful not to put them through yet another cancer journey. Mum just refused to believe I had 'cancer' and would rather assume that two tiny, but aggressive polyps had to be removed. Pradip became a self-appointed researcher in the field of oesophageal cancer, reading everything he could find and making contact with medical professionals known to us. Together we embraced this precarious journey, crying and laughing remaining strong in our faith, while facing the critical question "How long have I got?"

Multiple visits to hospitals for computerized tomography (CT) scan, endoscopic ultrasound scan (EUS) and a positron emission tomography (PET) scan for confirmation and staging purposes exerted relentless pressure upon all of us. Our anxiety intensified waiting for a phone call for the results. The nurse resounded the same words 'It is unclear' which compounded our apprehension, as we did not fully understand what 'unclear' meant. We were frustrated with yet another setback, when my appointment for an EUS at Watford hospital was delayed due to an equipment failure. During the procedure a week later, my throat was suitably numbed, and I clearly heard the words 'I can't find anything'. My metronomic mind swung between relief and doubt as it questioned 'where has it gone' or 'was it ever there in the first place', and more importantly, why I was going through this pendulum of uncertainty. The doctor repeated the EUS, without further numbing my throat, making this procedure very painful as I was choking. He later confirmed that the polyps were a stage 1b adenocarcinoma, albeit small and hopefully early, but poorly differentiated. In other words, small aggressive tumours, having the potential to spread rapidly and doing nothing was not an acceptable option. It was made clear that my prognosis would be poor without major surgery as one possible treatment option. One polyp was in the lower oesophagus and another at the junction of the oesophagus/stomach lining. From this report I could almost visualise the harrowing possibility of one travelling up through the oesophagus and another one on its way down to the stomach. For a moment the fear of the cancer spreading beyond this site became so real in my mind, but a glimmer of hope came from the doctor's parting words "You are very lucky, someone up there is looking after you.'

The presence of an aggressive cancer became a stark reality, which was hard to accept and what still remained was the dreadful uncertainty of treatment. Convincing my mother that there was a tumour and it was not going to disappear by itself was problematic, but because of her defiant nature, she was not going to accept defeat under any circumstances.

Badger, an eye-catching Alaskan Malamute with his master Paul by his side was at my door with his alluring stare, captivated me. His thick coat rubbed against me as I stroked him, feeling his strong sturdy body against my face. I shared a secret with him about my hospital visit for a PET scan that morning and my inner strength returned as I became better prepared to face my tests without fear. I shall never forget this moment of 'Badger therapy', which was more than a good omen.

BADGER THERAPY - PET Scan

Being at Mount Vernon Hospital in London for a PET scan was most upsetting seeing many patients at different stages receiving chemo and radio therapy. This brought flashbacks of our visits with my tormented brother undergoing chemotherapy at the Cross-Cancer Institute in Edmonton, Canada. I would open the precious piece of paper on which I had written the inspirational poem by Dr Robert L. Lynn "What cancer cannot do"[3]. Its opening question 'Can cancer conquer you?' would start an earnest conversation for him to look within for that strength which had nothing to do with his body cells. While holding his hand I would read each line slowly:

Cancer is so limited....

It cannot cripple love – for we are the embodiments of love

It cannot shatter hope – for hope is all we have

It cannot corrode faith – for faith is what we are made of

It cannot eat away peace – for peace begins in our minds

It cannot destroy confidence – for self- confidence is what our life is built on

It cannot kill friendship – for we are truly united with our nearest and dearest

---

[3] Cancer is so limited and other poems of Faith 2013 by Robert Lynn, ©Robert L. Lynn, 2007

It cannot shut out memories – for memories are the imprints of our journey

It cannot silence courage – for true courage keeps fear at bay

It cannot reduce eternal life – for that gift is in the hands of God

It cannot quench the Spirit – for the essence of life resides within us

I was asked to drink a large volume of sugar-based fluid, that would attract cancer cells, and the scan would identify their location. Given the evidence around linking diabetes with cancer, a question arose "Did my diabetes have a further bearing on the presence of cancer, especially as I had a familial link?"

The weekend was the longest wait for the results. Yet, another phone call repeated the same words 'We don't think it has spread but still unclear'. I feared being further stranded in the doldrums of uncertainty. Riding on the crest of an emotional roller coaster, we were oblivious of the creeping fatigue. We had no choice but to accept that life is unpredictable, but we managed to stay mindfully centred in the face of adversity. If we looked back, then time could end us; time cannot speak untruth and will not wait for anyone.

Elizabeth Kubler Ross, a Swiss psychiatrist explains that denial, anger, bargaining, depression and acceptance, are the rites of passage for anyone receiving a cancer diagnosis[4]. In this

---

[4] On Death & Dying: What the Dying Have to Teach Doctors, Nurses, Clergy & Their Own Families by Elisabeth Kubler-Ross and M D Ira Byock 2014

conundrum of fear, we manage to spirit a grain of survival into our starving minds where hope is born.

As we are all under the sentence of death, our hearts, like muffled drums are beating funeral marches to the grave. Some reach it late and some soon. It is at this junction of our life we realise the need for wise counsel to prepare us to meet what was to come - either life or death will prevail. While its timing is beyond our control, how we face this uncertainty depends on the choices we make

(Interpretation from the Bhagavatha Vahini by N. Kasturi)

FOUR

Eye of the cancer storm

*Cancer is only going to be a chapter in your life
and not the whole story*

- Joe Wasser

One misty morning, I found myself standing before the tall green cast-iron lamppost centred in Parker's Piece, Cambridge, which crosses two diagonal paths from the centre. Each pathway has its own end. The words 'Reality checkpoint' were not only inscribed at the base of the lamp post but also on my mind. This was home to me during my memorable days at Cambridge University. It provides the only light within a hundred meters or so and makes people feel safe at night walking across Parker's Piece.

This engraving had become a touchstone along my academic career and now it became part of my personal life. In the early hours of the morning I was awakened with a gentle whisper that cancer was not the problem to be solved, but a new *reality* to be experienced. The damp grass under my feet covered with its morning dew had a peculiar glow shining through the green underneath. The mist finally gave way to a rising sun emitting its golden rays bringing a comforting warmth. A flock of birds performed a triumphant aerobatic display and curiously soared low acknowledging my presence. The nascent sounds of this morning marked the freshness and the promising gifts of a new day, as if bequeathed from the heavens above. My thoughts turned to the time when rowing with the Hughes Hall novice team had taught me to be in rhythm where the individual, the team and the boat became part of one energy moving with precision in an atmosphere of calm and serenity. The River Cam was like a mother carrying its children in its flow, where we rowed with great spirit to the splashing sound of the oars and the scatter of the ducks in the dawn of each day. The cox was like a guardian angel instructing us in a gentle but firm voice keeping us on the straight and narrow as if navigating the course of the river and our lives. Echoes of the Eton Boat Song hummed in me with the words "We'll row for ever steady from stroke to bow and nothing in life shall sever the chains that are around us now...". I knew that we were all together in this journey as my thoughts turned to those who have gone before me and to those who were living with cancer. I now understood their painful passage as unpredictable events were ferrying my soul boat over life's sea. Will I be able to survive the vicissitudes of my journey?

Reality Checkpoint, Parker's Piece, Cambridge by Daksha Trivedi

Jenny G, a friend and a neighbour whom I had often seen in the village, adorning a colourful cap, carried a beaming smile with a glint in her eyes. Despite her ongoing battle with advanced cancer and chemotherapy, she walked with a purposeful determination overtaking me as I hobbled along on my crutches, after a road injury. Jenny showed more concern about my disability forgetting her own pain assuring me that before long I'd be climbing those steep hills. I saw the hard reality of her journey for a year and a half, during which time she continued to deteriorate as the cancer spread. But this did not stop her from enjoying her favourite activities – cooking, gardening, walking and having a grand family holiday. She was not only a scientist but also held a private pilot's licence and her love for flying stayed with her till the end. Always staying on the sunny side of the street, her last words to me were "Do not have any sense of guilt, we did not invite this disease". I learnt that one can live well until the end is nigh.

The petite Diana with a Mona Lisa smile who moved energetically to the music of Neapolitan Tarantella was a great source of inspiration at our international folk-dance club. She had undergone drastic surgery with radio and chemotherapy for bowel cancer but resolved to participate with passion in all her activities including tennis, which enabled her to continue to live life to the full. The notion of giving up or slowing down was not in her mindset and today three years on she remains cancer free. Recurring thoughts of 'How long have I got' ..'is it spreading' would sometimes creep up and trouble me, but meeting people who found ways of savouring each day at a time, inspired me to live well in the moment.

Memories of Lynne Sparkes, the bright and cheerful mayor of Welwyn and Hatfield remain with me to this date. She championed the annual multicultural event where people came together from different faiths to share songs of praise. We continued to work together promoting interfaith dialogue and witnessed the magic of people coming together celebrating life's unity in diversity. While waiting for my PET scan, I received the heart-breaking news that Lynne had passed away unexpectedly from a rare form of cancer. The unpredictable nature of cancer made me appreciate the value and fragility of life.

My very close friend, Nirmala, unable to travel on our pilgrimage to India, due to a sudden onset of swallowing difficulties, was subsequently diagnosed with advanced oesophageal cancer. Greatly saddened by her loss, and now having a similar diagnosis, her suffering became even more real to me. I learnt the most valuable lesson, that contemplating on death, which was only an incident in life was a complete waste of the present moment whereas contemplating on loving memories made every moment precious.

Closer to home, my uncle, a colourful character and a teacher by profession always carried a pedagogical approach to life. Conversations with him often ended with educational statements, sometimes challenging my assertions for a lively banter and suddenly breaking into a rendition of romantic songs from old Hindi movies. It was sad to see this otherwise gregarious person living painfully and severely restricted with his cancer for some years. His eyes would light up when we visited him and ruminated over his young days in Nairobi, while courageously accepting his gradual deterioration.

My deepest admiration for him was that he lived life to the full and remained bonded with all whom he loved so well.

A wise old friend, Mr Kapoor Shah always made time for me and our regular conversations were often Socratic, unravelling the mysteries of daily life sometimes with great amusement. Deeply affected by the loss of his loving wife to cancer, he seemed to lose his will to live and sadly he was diagnosed with myeloma, a form of bone cancer. We both agreed that even if one's body is failing; the mind can still be a source of hope for others. Despite many health difficulties, he continued to help many troubled souls in their hour of need. He never lost his faith in God and in his final moments had the sudden insight to call me by his bedside. His last words to me were "Daksha, exercise and lose weight". Nothing more was exchanged with anyone, and he breathed his last breath soon after. A wise nurturer till the end, encouraging me to live well. The most pertinent message he gave me those ten years ago was that we can face any eventuality with fortitude and faith.

We are so immersed in the physical challenges that the mental trauma remains underestimated, not quantifiable and undetected. Neuroscientists refer to this as 'inattentional blindness' which can lead to disastrous consequences. Life is far more than understanding it through formulaic equations and quantifying it in terms of how long we will survive. It is obvious that we will continue to live until we die, but it is more important to consider *how* we will live rather than how long. It was not by chance alone that these inspiring souls were part of my life. Having cancer did not separate us but created genuine bonds of curative love, far beyond my expectations.

I have cancer...the cancer does NOT have me..." It does not possess the whole of me, and there is a large part of me that will remain strong and resilient to rise like the Phoenix.

FIVE

From fear to hope

Courage is resistance to fear, mastery of fear,
not absence of fear
- **Mark Twain**

I could instantly sense that the doctor was in a dilemma of how
to convey the findings of my biopsy to me. Her demeanour was
impersonal, as she distanced herself and gave me the results. My
breathing became shallow as I heard her words "I am a locum
consultant and I have just been brought in today only to give you
this news". My husband and I were in tears and no one was there to
comfort us. Later, the nurse advised me to inform my employers and
make a five- year plan. Knowing nothing about options for treatment
or even the prognosis, the fear of facing the absolutely unknown,
was a fate worse than death. I genuinely felt that I shouldn't have
got the news in the way I did. Perhaps feeling alone, forced me to
turn inwards and find my own strength in order to deal with my
deepest of fears. I could not help asking the question "why me?".

Overcoming fear is something that we all have to do at some point
when we are faced with obstacles that stand in our way. We can
measure body symptoms and physiological parameters, but the
power of fear, hope or courage are immeasurable. What is it that
we fear? Can we ever escape fear? We are afraid to fail, afraid
to lose, therefore afraid to live and finally afraid to die. We are so
conditioned into a daily pattern of doing what is expected of us that

we never see the invisible gorilla rampaging in our subconscious juggling with doubts and fears. This has a crippling effect on us in every way, and fear is believed to be the most chronic disease of our time.

My cancer diagnosis became pivotal in my efforts to overcome fear. Every day we take a gamble on life, not knowing the outcome, but always hoping to win. The magic penny I held so tightly in my hand had hope on one side and fear on the other, and it was time for me to flip the coin in this matter of life and death. Instead of being paralysed by fear about what could happen, I had to learn to transcend each of my fears. I believed I would be guided by my inner spirit to deal with the sum of all my fears and in doing so, my inner strength grew. Whilst these demons did not disappear, they did lose their dominion over me, giving me courage to move forward despite their lurking presence. A patient with an early stage cancer *can* have a better chance of survival after surgery so I placed all my faith into this one chance, still not knowing the extent of spread until surgery.

While I waited for my PET scan, looking into the eyes of the cancer patients, I could sense their deepest fears. The room was filled with an eerie silence and I knew from this that my battle was not only against cancer, but to fight the fear. Each person must have held a wish known only to them. I wished to have enough time to do something worthwhile with God's presence in my life. The vicious circle of worry and doubts forced me to find ways of living in the present. It was like taking a giant leap from the highest peak to the inviting calm of the lake not knowing if the jagged rocks beneath will kill you. The fear comes without warning, and feeling it is one thing but to discover why it is there and how to deal with it requires courage.

It is well documented that stressful thinking can adversely affect our health, and conversely positive and self- healing thoughts are known to produce favourable effects, particularly on the immune system. Our thoughts and feelings are known to produce biological and behavioural differences, and perhaps this could go some way towards explaining the differences in the manifestation of the same disease in both my brother and me.

It is believed that mental images and feelings leave an imprint of disease in our cells, possibly by activating specific genes that can produce diseased or healthy cells. Releasing emotional pain is also known to have a positive effect on our health. Dwelling on our illness is normal, as we cannot forget about the cancer within us. Therefore, I developed my own method of healing, based on experiential evidence and continued to work on my fears, thoughts, beliefs and attitudes to sustain a positive mind-set. In this way, I could keep my natural fears and anxieties at bay, allowing hope to flourish. As I faced up to them, I understood them better and was able to let go. They shook me and pointed me to my brave self as fear and courage recited a soliloquy to my soul.

Many like me, who are intensively target driven in the world of academia, conducting high quality research and competing for research grants are on a treadmill ignoring their own needs. Having cancer flagged up an ultimatum to transform my lifestyle and to harmonise my mental, emotional and spiritual faculties. I needed a new *raison d'etre that* would mean more to me than anything else in the world. Armed with this powerful *intention* in one hand and an unquestioning belief in the other, I prepared myself with courage to conquer this force of illness and my close call with the grim reaper.

As I lay in my bed, I heard my mother's soft voice praying "Tamaso maa jyotir gamaya. O lead us from darkness to light" At that moment, hope borne out of desperation, became the most powerful drug with no side effects.

Though my last moments with my brother were heart wrenching, I said to him "Don't blame yourself, the cancer was not your fault". I could see that he had summoned the strong spirit within him, replacing months of fear and anguish. Even with sadness in his eyes, his smile revealed that something beautiful awaited him. Our last doorstep farewell filled us both with pure light, love and hope.

Belief is the fuel that determines where we can be in this life's spectrum between health and disease. Many of us see only the black dots in our life, we do not see the vast spaces surrounding the black dots. Our belief in the power of hope and wellbeing, must be greater than in the power of illness.

> "Hope" is the thing with feathers -
> That perches in the soul -
> And sings the tune without the words -
> And never stops - at all -
>
> And sweetest - in the Gale - is heard -
> And sore must be the storm -
> That could abash the little Bird
> That kept so many warm -
>
> I've heard it in the chillest land -
> And on the strangest Sea -
> Yet - never - in Extremity,
> It asked a crumb - of me.
>
> **Emily Dickinson**

This poem aptly conveys to me that hope is embedded in our hearts, giving us the courage to persevere through adversity, asking nothing in return.

SIX

Thinking about cancer

It's a disease, NOT a decision

Cancer does not discriminate between the prince and the pauper, a politician and a physician, or a baker and a candlestick maker, for it knows no bounds. This chronic disease accounts for more than a quarter (28%) of all deaths in the UK, with around 165,000 cancer deaths every year, which means 450 every day. One in two people will develop cancer at some point in their lives, according to the Cancer Research UK although the overall cancer survival rates are improving with early detection.

I knew that oesophageal cancer was aggressive and clearly not the best one to have with an overall 5- year survival rate from around 5-30% in patients who are amenable to treatment. Being from an Asian background my concern increased as I discovered that this type of cancer was relatively uncommon (3% of all cancers), particularly in women (31% of cases) compared with men (69% of cases), and less prevalent in Asians (age standardised rates 2.5-4.5 per 100, 000) than in white people (age standardised rates 5.5 to 5.7 per 100,000)[5]. I stumbled upon evidence from a large Nordic twin study of cancer which included 200, 000 twins[6]. It was estimated

[5] National Cancer Intelligence Network and Cancer Research UK, 2009 Cancer Incidence and Survival by Major Ethnic Group, England, 2002-2006

[6] Lorelei A. Mucci et al on behalf of the Nordic Twin Study of Cancer (NorTwinCan) collaboration. Familial risk and heritability of cancer among twins in Nordic countries. JAMA, January 5, 2016 DOI: 10.1001/jama.2015.17703

that when one fraternal twin sibling was diagnosed with cancer, there was an excess risk of 37% in the co-twin of getting cancer.

Together with this familial risk a host of other factors may be involved but the causality remains equivocal and I needed to think more about why and how cancer happens. We know that we are made up of millions of cells, and cancer can start with one or more cells and their growth is controlled by signals from our cells. It is not clear how and when this becomes faulty, but the DNA code in our genes directs the cells' behaviour. Altered genes or mutations would mean that our cell(s) no longer understand the instructions and begin to grow.

Berenblum and Schubik in 1949[7] explained the process of carcinogenesis (how cancer is formed), which is supported by several studies. The modus operandi includes three stages. In the first stage the cell's genetic component undergoes an irreversible change, followed by promotion where these cells that are triggered, proliferate and grow abnormally; and progression, where the cells separate from the initial tumour site and attack the nearby tissues.

Bishop, the Nobel Prize winner stated in 1982 that *"Normal cells may bear the seeds of their own destruction in the form of cancer genes. The activities of these genes may represent the final common pathway by which many carcinogens act. **Cancer genes may not be unwanted guests but essential constituents of the cell's***

---

[7] Berenblum I, Shubik P An experimental study of the initiating state of carcinogenesis, and a re-examination of the somatic cell mutation theory of cancer. Br J Cancer. 1949 Mar;3(1):109-18.

genetic apparatus, betraying the cell only when their structure or control is distributed by carcinogens"[8]

Based on Bishop's statement, if cancer did originate from the cells within our body, then it would make sense to direct my healing efforts at the cellular level. So, the question arises "are we ill or are we healthy or are we both at the same time?" In Buddhism, sickness is often perceived as a disturbance, with illness manifesting from within. We are all genetically different and our needs are constantly changing, so we need to go beyond a preconceived model of health care to one that will treat the whole patient, and not just the disease. At the molecular biology level, we know that the cells in our bodies are constantly ageing and are receiving harmful carcinogens, such as UV radiation and many pollutants. It is necessary for us to eliminate those harmful cancerous cells and surgery can remove cancerous tissues, but can it possibly deal with the signalling mechanisms that make cells proliferate abnormally? As cancer cells are intrinsically part of our own cellular family, is it therefore possible for us to 'treat' the harmful cells back to their benign natural state? These questions, rhetorical in nature, provide some degree of consolation in our need to reason why this has happened to us.

I had a vague understanding and acceptance of the notion of karma (thought, word and deed) and its consequences from my Hindu background. What did make sense to me was that karma, the law of cause and effect states that every action will generate a force or energy that will subsequently affect us. Like the force of gravity

---

[8] J.M. Bishop: In Oncogenes. Scientific American, 1982, 246, 80-92

that is certainly invisible, its effects are felt. In a similar manner, the karmic forces which are latent do manifest in our lives. We readily accept Sir Isaac Newton's law, "Every action has an equal and opposite reaction," yet we find it difficult to fully accept the science and wisdom of the law of karma.

If I were to believe that my diagnosis was a 'karmic boomerang" and that no one can escape its consequences, then there must be a way of negating or minimising the impact on my life. Thinking about my twin brother who also had a primary diagnosis of cancer of the lower oesophagus, I needed to somehow accept both the genetic predisposition *and* the effects of karmic consequences. From birth to adulthood, our paths were not dissimilar including our education. Though we received the same initial diagnosis, albeit at a different time, our 'karmic' lifestyles varied as did our individual cancer journeys. My karmic connection with him had ended and being fraternal twins, the separation was inevitable in this life. He continues his journey without looking back leaving his past behind; and I continue looking forward learning from my past.

It is hypothesised that the human genome and the theory of karma are intricately linked (Times of India, 29 October 2005). The geneticist, Dean Hamer states in the article that dormant genes could be activated by changes in our lifestyles. Karma does not necessarily determine our destiny as we do have the opportunity to influence its effects.

Having understood this principle, I placed all my hopes for a good outcome which required a combination of conventional and complimentary therapies. Even if we do not fully understand the principle of 'cause and effect', we can certainly agree that increased stress, anxiety and poor lifestyle can not only affect our immune response to disease, but also contribute to psychosomatic symptoms. Anxiety and stress can also trigger or worsen symptoms related to Gastroesophageal reflux disease, or GERD which is a risk factor for gastro intestinal cancer. Stress can reduce the production of prostaglandins (group of lipids) which normally protect the stomach from acid build up.

We can never underestimate the power of our intention in determining the outcome of our efforts, especially where our health is concerned. By consciously directing all my energies on my well-being I learnt to deal with my 'dis-ease' to restore balance in my life. I had never envisaged that this event would become my mentor, without which I would have been in a boat without a paddle.

Cancer be not so proud, for thou do not know the will of God. Nor art thou the Lord of time. When I unleash the invincible power within me, I become the master of my destiny

SEVEN

Take a deep breath

For breath is life, and if you breathe well you will live long on earth

- Sanskrit Proverb

Words resounding 'It's all over 'paralysed me until a gentle but firm voice whispered, "It's not over, until the fat lady sings!'

I was always aware of the health benefits of the ancient noble path of mindful meditation which now became a way of life for me. Both my personal and professional life merged in a state of quintessential mindfulness which I held in thoughtful equipoise. The more I practised this art, the more effortless it became, and it soothed the vulnerable parts of me with an incandescent energy. During the practice of Reiki energy healing I learnt the art of conscious breathing, directing my awareness into each breath and sending it to every part of me, which is known as So-hum breathing (I am that, one with the Universe). When interrupted by any random thought I would acknowledge it and return to my mindful breathing, which tamed my untutored mind. In this refreshing nowness where pain, fear and anxiety ceased to possess me, my mind and body became synchronised to the rhythm of my breath. This guides us to remain in the present moment so that we do not miss that precious time given to us. The practice is known to reduce stress and has a favourable effect on our health, biochemistry, physiology, immune function and psychological well-being, through the changes in the neurological pathways which modify fear and anxiety. Dr David Hamilton has pulled together a strong evidence base for the connection between mind, body and spirit that influences our health at every level[9]. Having a healthy mind for a healthy body right through to the cellular level where my disease had found a home, was therefore of utmost importance to me.

Meditation creates the ambiance within us revealing questions that awaken us to the reality we are facing in a more balanced and an emotionally stable manner. One could say we are connecting to our higher consciousness or higher self which guides us to deal with life's events.

I remember vividly, gently submerging into the depths of the Indian Ocean, off the coast of Goa where I lost myself in the blue nowhere as my body took the shape of water. All that remained was conscious breathing dissolving expectations, thoughts or worries. The buoyancy of moving in various directions and floating as well as breathing rhythmically in this vastness brought a heavenly experience, a new free will without limitations. With every breath I understood this gift of life and the reason for being alive with yet another day to swim with the dolphins.

---

[9] It's The Thought That Counts: Why Mind Over Matter Really Works by David R. Hamilton, Ph.D

Blue diving...Breathe....

Photo of Valentine Thomas, taken by Justin Baluch.

In our desperate search for answers, we often explore various practices. Some call it prayer or conversing with God, others call it being in contemplation with the inner spirit. Whichever path we choose, we must be open to receive inner guidance. Walking in the woods I embraced my time of solitude absorbing the beauty of nature and its healing, sitting in church or any place of worship- all these became my sanctum sanctorum. I felt connected to something bigger than myself transforming from a limited being to a limitless spirit. These were my introspective moments, without judgement, right or wrong, good or bad, but just being in a state of acceptance and goodness. Psychologists often refer to these as transpersonal moments and spiritual seekers refer to these as connecting with the divine. Neuroscience has indicated that the practice of meditation changes the balance of the stress related hormones, such as epinephrine and over a period of time, alters aspects of our brain anatomy, improving concentration of the mind and establishing a constant integrated awareness.

We can often become hypervigilant where we are stuck in an obsessive mode, perceive every change as a threat and over analyse every situation searching for a place of safety. Though we are aware of such destructive behaviours, we are unable to control them. Our survival brain is constantly bombarding the body at the cellular level pleading for a safe haven and these signals are psychological in nature based on our inherent fears. We end up in a state of helplessness, unable to take risks to get us out of difficult situations. Each one of us has the ability to access our inner guide or sometimes referred to as the guru of our mind, body and spirit. Being still, allowed me to access this inner wisdom thereby regulating my response to cancer, such that I moved from anger and resentment to a place of serenity. This greatly reduced my stress response to life's unexpected events and my perception began to shift to things that were more important in life than being caught up in mundane living. I learnt to take the richness from every experience, discovering joy in the smallest moments and not taking my present life for granted.

So, whilst death was a real possibility, I focused on what I could control and *letting go* of everything beyond my control. I gained a better sense of my reality going beyond the false notions about how life should be. Vagaries of the mind about what life could have been, should have been or even might be, served no purpose. I began to *breathe* life into every experience, no matter how daunting it may seem.

As I walked back home one afternoon, I noticed that my shadow was in front of me, as if I was walking towards darkness. Cancer had obscured the light from my life and here I made a choice to face the sun even through the clouds of despair.

Our breath is the equilibrium of life from the moment we are born. Its metronomic rhythm creates harmony within us. It transcends what is fragile and uncertain. We learn to observe our life as it happens, accepting our situation without judgement or struggle.

Breath of Life
I breathe in All That is –
Awareness expanding
to take everything in,
as if my heart beats
the world into being

From the unnamed
vastness beneath the
mind, I breathe my
way to wholeness
and healing

Inhalation, Exhalation.
Each breath a "yes",
and a letting go,
a journey, and a
coming home

**- Danna Faulds from her book Go In and In: Poems from the
Heart of Yoga**

EIGHT

Healing embraced

Healing does not mean the damage never existed.
It means the damage no longer controls our lives
- Akshay Dubey

Embodied in the eastern traditions, is the ancient belief of a universal life sustaining force described as Qi (chee) or prana or universal energy, without which we cannot function. This energy flow nourishes our vital organs and if for any reason, the Qi is blocked, our cells are starved of the life force and illness can ensue. This knowledge and practice would be vital as I created my own self-healing plan.

Hippocrates, the father of medicine declared that natural forces within us are the true healers of disease. Being a Reiki practitioner, I came across cancer patients who reported a number of health benefits. Some were unable to engage possibly due to lack of focus, agitation and anxiety and holding on to their fears which could result in blocking their energy flow, like an obstruction in the vessels restricting the blood flow damaging the heart or other organs. Stimulating the Qi through holistic healing can dissolve these blockages. Every part of us is in a vibrational energy field, and healing targets those areas which regulate our energy centres (chakras). Mindful breathing allows us to access our own Qi enabling it to flow through the cells, tissues and organs.

Medical treatment, diet and exercise all have their place in improving health, but so does the power of our intentions. They create the vibrations conducive for healing to take place. I became open to receiving therapy that would restore my natural flow of Qi, aware of the need to release or unblock many stored emotions. It is well known that stored negative emotions can further perpetuate illness, in the same way as stored cholesterol can cause atheroma and heart disease. At the seat of an inflamed mind lie stored emotional and psychological traumas from the past which disturb us today and desperately need healing. I received Reiki energy healing[10] regularly and together with mindful meditation I learnt the art of self-healing. Before long, I was in an equilibrium of good vibrational energy in preparation for my treatment.

Apollo, the Greek God of music has graced us with healing harmonies and knowing that music has a beneficial effect on our health through neuropeptides, I filled myself with the soothing sounds of invigorating music. If negative thoughts swamped my mind, draining away vital energy, I would use creative visualisation for what I wanted to manifest. Whenever I attended clinics or took medications, I visualised with purpose a picture of ideal health. During my daily walks, I soaked up the glory of nature's colours and embraced the trees melting away into their rugged trunks, feeling the soft touch of their overhanging branches. This sacred moment transcended the burden of uncertainty, but which reignited in me the lust for life with a greater intensity than ever before.

---

[10] Healing from Falguni Bhatt, Malini Rawal, Vina Mistry, Brother Hoe Lim (Reiki practitioners)

Tai Chi, a form of moving and breathing meditation also helped me to focus on inner calmness necessary to enable a healing energy flow. This practice was recommended even before surgery to get me in a ready state with regard to muscular flexibility and strengthening, as the body would be subjected to rigid surgical procedures. Whilst there does not appear to be robust evidence on what works, there are many patients who have reported benefits of reduced stress levels and an improved immune function.

I adhered to my exercise programme given to me by my referral coordinator. Physical activity is known to release endorphins[11] and other neurotransmitters[12] which can not only reduce anxiety and depression but also inflammation.

Creating an 'ideal diet' would be desirable in this process, and after researching respectable websites and documented case studies, I experienced the goodness of colourful fresh fruit and vegetable smoothies and I also increased my protein intake and foods known to further enhance my immune system.

We are often unaware of the subtle effects of vibrations on our health. Here, vibrational medicines also have a place in our healing. In this system vibrations in the form of high frequency electromagnetic waves are administered in a solid or liquid substance, for example, tiny sugar pills or water. They are neutral homeopathic like pills, but without any chemical components, set to the required vibrational

---

[11] Group of hormones secreted in the brain and nervous system

[12] Chemical messengers that transmit signals between neurons, or nerve cells, and other cells in the body.

frequency for a particular medical condition. Sai vibrionics, a system of healing also provided a means to balance my vital energies which improved my overall health. It acts as a catalyst to awaken the power of inner healing at physical, mental, emotional, and spiritual levels.

Ayurvedic medicine, an ancient whole-body healing system, originating in India over 3,000 years ago is being increasingly used in the treatment of various ailments. It has at its core, a commonly held belief that our health is influenced by a fine balance between the mind, body and spirit. Many have reported great benefits on their health. Vani Moodley, a qualified practitioner provided me with advice on simple home remedies to alleviate some of my symptoms during recovery.

Embracing both allopathic and holistic medicine, *and* being receptive, I learnt intuitively to listen to my mind and body, paying close attention to every cell, tissue, organ and nerve, and putting all my focused awareness to specific areas that needed healing. It is believed that every cell in our body has an innate intelligence to heal. Dr Sondra Barret in her intriguing work 'Secrets of Your Cells: Discovering Your Body's Inner Intelligence' takes us through the inner realms of our cellular universe. Our cells are not just there by chance but are living units of energy which together form a safe haven.

During my guided self-healing meditation, I was able to consciously direct my breath to these areas, gently releasing the tension in these parts with my outgoing breath. Each breath was like water, fresh and cleansing, flowing freely into my lungs and bringing nourishment to the mind, body and spirit. Using Louise Hay's health-giving affirmations in a guided meditation was particularly calming and beneficial. I would drift off to sleep and be awakened in the morning with more positive, uplifting and an exhilarating energy that conveyed 'you *can* heal your life'! Louise Hay lived well for thirty years after a cancer diagnosis, which bears testament to the power of self-healing.

Waiting for results and decisions around my treatment, taught me to allow celestial healing in every way where needed. Thus, started a process of *cleansing* as I learnt to *activate* my energy flow through physical exercise, and mindful meditation. I focused on my breath in the present without distraction from the past or the future. With practice, I felt the universal life force in my breath infusing healing oxygen to all my cells. I discarded the once important 'to do list' and the stories of all my yesterdays. As I sensed the affirmations within me, I became convinced of the vital healing potential of my body.

Next day would be different and delivered a feeling of optimism that had eluded me for so long but which I received as a welcome stranger. I was not sure that today would be any better than yesterday, but this time that we had gained would give birth to a spark of hope.

The fountain of energy that is within us is stronger than a million suns. It comes to heal us when we connect to the Source. We just need to provide everything our bodies need. We then truly appreciate our body's innate ability to heal us.

May You Be Well

May you be well.
May you be cleansed and purified
Of all that isn't health.
May every cell in your body
Wake up and fight.
May the powerful light of healing
Move into every part of you.
May you return to being purely you.
May you be well.

© By Joanna Fuchs

NINE

Every thought counts

*Man creates his own reality by tuning
into the appropriate channel of the
all-pervading energy*

How often do we come across the statement "It's the thought that counts"? It usually refers to giving and receiving gifts, placing value on the intention and the thought behind the action. What we think becomes our reality and psychologists refer to this as the neuroimaginary world. In other words, we create our world from our thoughts.

Managing my thoughts, feelings and sensations during my daily activities with an increasing kinesthetic awareness brought an inimitable lightness to my life. This enabled me to cope with the complex nature of my condition with a greater sense of detachment. Cancer may still be a part of me but would not define me.

We all live in an interconnected world, even though we perceive ourselves as separate individual entities. Along the way, our spiritual development expands our consciousness and we begin to transcend the notion of separateness. In this awakened state, we experience genuine feelings of empathy and love for ourselves and others.

Our thoughts come from our conscious mind, and impress upon our subconscious mind, which has the 'apps' that produce our habitual patterns. I became acutely aware that every thought carries its own vibrational energy which influences our daily life. Mastering the itinerant mind becomes necessary to avoid negative thoughts which steal our inner peace. Using the creative powers of the subconscious mind, I learnt to channel only positive thoughts to aid my own healing. We accept that our thoughts and emotions affect our metabolism, and the release of stress hormones such as cortisol affecting our immune system and its ability to control inflammation. Scientists have shown that even placebos can produce powerful effects generated by expectations at both the conscious or the subconscious level. Thoughts do indeed have a magnetic power, whereby we draw to ourselves that which we think of constantly.

There are numerous reports of people using the power of affirmations and prayers for their positive outcomes. It is a mystery why we pray but do not always get the expected result. And why do different patients with the same condition have different outcomes? Some recover and others do not, some resign to their inexorable fate, gradually reducing contact with the outside world, while others seem to go beyond the diagnosis and their given prognosis to live as fully as they can.

The British Medical Journal (2001)[13] reporting on the beneficial effects of prayer, showed that those who prayed *effectively* improved breathing and increased oxygenated blood flow to the heart. It has also been associated with good health, quality of life, and reduced psychological distress. The need to pray exists in every faith with

[13] Bernardi L et al., BMJ. 2001 Dec 22-29;323(7327):1446-9.

the belief that we are drawing on a source of all pervading universal energy. I became even more aware than before that my prayers were indeed my thoughts and desires which needed to be specific, focused and had a declaration of intent. This process may not have the desired effect if the conscious mind wants to be cured but at the sub conscious level, fears and doubts prevail.

In the case of my twin brother, his face revealed his thoughts understandably swinging like a pendulum between life and death, and hope and despair. Whilst he welcomed healing prayers from family and friends, his doubts would prevail. However, he was surprised at the improvement of his quality of life at times when he had a positive and a receptive mindset. Even though a bad prognosis is given by the medical team, each day can be fulfilling and different irrespective of the timeline. We often come across people who have defied the given timelines for survival and lived to tell the tale.

Impressing the creative power of positive thoughts on the subconscious mind requires us to accept that whilst death is a possibility, we do have the power to improve our quality of life and well-being. In doing so, we do not allow fearful thoughts to control us, and become rooted in our subconscious mind. Whenever fear and anxiety broached my mind, I immediately replaced these with affirmations of healing and restoration, allowing every cell to vibrate in the energy of my breath and thoughts. These were my conversations with the divine spirit within me. I would launch into a monologue about seeing myself free from this affliction. My subconscious mind received my desire to be restored so that I could be of service to those in need. The practice that helped manifest wholeness in my life was not without challenges and I developed at my own pace. I am now convinced that when we learn to think in new ways, our brain cells rearrange themselves to process this new information.

We have the free will to choose a new thought and when we do so, we begin to live in this new environment. Here, we experience a synergetic resonance with the universal vibrational energy which continues to reverberate within us. Using affirmations or prayers I was placing my needs into this vibrational field of energy, believing truly that they would manifest in an appropriate manner, beyond human understanding. It is a mystery how the good and godly came into my life at this time with prayers of hope and healing as if my desires and thoughts were received by the universal consciousness.

My friends in Christ held special prayers creating a cornerstone for my life to be renewed. Whilst I was educated in a predominantly Christian school in Nairobi, I also learnt to embrace the teachings from all other faiths. Pastor Raleigh and his wife Alcy from South Africa declared in His name that my recovery would be full and complete. Father Tom sent me healing prayers affirming that I still had a purpose on this earth as long as I had breath in my body. Dr Andreas Braun, my colleague and friend, from the International Church in Luton, now living in Finland, prayed ardently that God's mercy and love would protect me and my family. Our niece Hema Dionne Trivedi from the Mosaic church in Coventry formed her own prayer group for my healing, led by a pastor who proclaimed that I would soon give a testimony of God's intervention in my life.

They brought a special scriptural message "*I have loved you with an everlasting love; I have drawn you with unfailing kindness. I will build you up again, and you...will be rebuilt (Jeremiah 31:3-4, NIV).*

Our dear friends from the North Hertfordshire and Welwyn Hatfield interfaith groups from various beliefs and traditions included me in their combined prayers. Spiritual aspirants from the multi faith Sai Baba centres, both nationally and internationally, all prayed to the one omnipresent Divine who resides in each one of us. I genuinely felt surrounded by such positive energy full of loving empathy that I moved from having just faith to implicit trust in my inner self. It was no longer just about cure, but more about not being alone which was comforting and knowing that whatever happens will be for my overall good. In this spirit of surrender, I felt the lightness of being one with my inner spirit in a liberating experience. In the words of Hippocrates, "Healing is a matter of time, but it is sometimes also a matter of opportunity".

In our solitude, when we stop thinking, our mind is in a different place. It becomes a vessel to receive profound insights that will liberate us from our deeply pained state to accepting the reality of our situation. "Our thoughts and destiny are interconnected" (Sathya Sai Baba)

TEN

Preparing to meet my fate

In the planning stage of your treatment, do not plan your ending

The long night before my appointment with the lead surgeon was the darkest of my life filled with mixed emotions. Judgement day was looming when I would be served the final decision of my suitability for treatment. Would I endure the same fate as my brother whose cancer was inoperable? It was a panoramic night of a thousand stars in an inky black sky and I wondered where people went after they passed over. Perhaps these beautiful souls that once dwelt on this earth are now fulfilling their purpose according to the laws of the spirit world. In my heart, I felt as if I was being guided by them to face my tomorrow. Despite all the lessons learnt along my spiritual journey, I was not infallible, and I witnessed my own vulnerability to the challenges that befell me.

Though I felt uneasy, my health checks were conducted in a routine and a clinical manner. Patients and their families waited expectantly and each time the nurse came out all heads looked up hoping it was their turn. Some bided time by tapping their feet to music from their earphones, others just stared at the clock nervously as if they had an inkling of what was to come. Before a wave of anxiety could overcome me, I managed to practise subtle breathing exercises to help me relax. Lost in this quiet and tense atmosphere, I was jolted upon hearing my name and quickly rose to my feet as the nurse escorted us to a side room from which we could hear my name being mentioned several times. Soon after, the surgeon, Mr Al-Bahrani, accompanied by the cancer nurse specialist and the dietician, entered with a charismatic smile to convey his decision, which he did with such a dramatic proficiency, almost worthy of a scene from a hospital drama. I felt he could deliver the worst news making the patient feel that it is not as bad as it seems! He emanated an aura of goodness, that told me he was certainly a gifted man.

"Do you know why you are here?" he asked with probing eyes. I nodded, as my pent-up feelings burst into searching questions for there had been little opportunity to discuss this matter with anyone. He requested me to wait patiently until he had finished, and I hoped that I would get the answers from the information he was providing. I had to wait one more hour on top of the 12 weeks from diagnosis and felt worthy of a champion's medal in patience. My fears resurfaced reaching a pinnacle when his voice delivered the words 'I am offering you a *possible* curative surgery'. Hope emerged from the depths of my despair. My tears that I had held back for so long burst into a torrent, thanking God for this moment.

Mr Al-Bahrani drew a detailed schema of an esophagectomy, which would involve a nine-hour radical surgery to remove my oesophagus. This procedure would mean going through my abdomen, chest wall and ribs, collapsing my lung and restructuring my stomach into a long tube starting in my chest to replace the removed oesophagus. In no uncertain terms, he reiterated the seriousness of this major procedure and gave me grim statistics on complications such as bleeding, infection and sepsis, anastomosis leak, lung failure and fatality. Because the scans were somewhat unclear, it was difficult to determine the extent of spread. Should I agree to surgery, he would scan my nearby organs first and if there was any suggestion of lesions beyond the oesophagus, he would stop, close me up and not proceed further. If I did not agree to this, it would only be a few months at best before I would have swallowing difficulties and little else could be done for me. In other words, my chances of survival without surgery were poor. On the other hand, the aftermath from surgery with its lasting implications on food management would be extremely challenging. Being shaken up, it took me a while to process the severity of what was being proposed.

My stomach churned with agony as I felt so alone being asked to hand over my life to the surgical team. As I agreed to this life-threatening surgery, I wept like a lost child, my life no longer being my own. Time stood still and all I could hear were muffled voices in the background. I held Pradip's hand and looked away from the surgeon as everything felt surreal. "Do you want me to stop?" I heard the surgeon, bringing me back to the moment. His gaze was so intense but confident, even though I tried to avert his scrutiny.

We were also informed that my family should not become alarmed at seeing me post operatively in intensive care, all wired up and not being able to recognise me. From then on, we would go with each day at a time to help me recover. The shock of all this spilled over into black humour when the mortality risks were being discussed as my husband quipped "You need to make sure she lives otherwise you don't get paid, right?" "Oh, I get paid anyway" replied the surgeon and the room filled with gallows humour. "Can you do this?" Pradip asked. The surgeon looked at him assertively and said he would not offer this procedure otherwise. He did add though that it was rare to have something identified like this without any presenting symptoms. Without hesitation the surgeon added "Someone up there is looking after you", a phrase that was often repeated by those charged to look after me.

Why was I referred in the first place? I could only put it down to my GP having an insight given my family history. Looking back, I often wonder whether an intuitive moment by a doctor when presented with a patient without major or obvious symptoms tells of a divine instruction to act. The timing of the test was most fortuitous, and I discovered later that at the back of my doctor's mind was indeed my brother's cancer.

Uncertainty continued to linger as any sign of spread beyond the oesophagus would mean surgery coming to an abrupt end, even after being suitably fit for surgery.

We travelled home in silent contemplation reflecting on the events of the day, holding firmly the comprehensive information booklet given to us by Mr Al-Bahrani who had explained assiduously all the procedures involved. I was clearly not out of the woods yet, my thoughts creating one weeping symphony after another. We were like sunflowers that follow the sun, but on cloudy days we face each other and share our strength. We were now on a road to a place from which we could never come back to where we were.

The force of circumstance brings us amidst a myriad of human experiences. We move from an immured place of solitude to a place where hope flourishes. When a hand is held out to us, we will take it.

Invictus

Out of the night that covers me,
Black as th e pit from pole to pole,
I thank whatever gods may be
For my unconquerable soul.

In the fell clutch of circumstance
I have not winced nor cried aloud.
Under the bludgeonings of chance
My head is bloody, but unbowed.

Beyond this place of wrath and tears
Looms but the Horror of the shade,
And yet the menace of the years
Finds and shall find me unafraid.

It matters not how strait the gate,
How charged with punishments the scroll,
I am the master of my fate,
I am the captain of my soul.

-William Ernest Henley

ELEVEN

It's time to get fit

It's not only the strength of the body that counts but also the strength of the spirit

The persistent voice inside me like that of an army training instructor yelled at me to keep moving as I huffed and puffed on the cardio pulmonary exercise testing machine. When the figures on the monitor exceeded the level required, I heard "Well done" with great aplomb and to the sound of a loud applause. It did not surprise me that I had passed the fitness test and though I was a diabetic and somewhat overweight, walking had been my past time for many years. This was the first step on a steep and rocky path of endurance with still a long way to go.

Our holiday to Madeira with Rajiv and Priti, which had been pre-booked before my diagnosis now became uncertain. With great anticipation, they were looking forward to this time to celebrate my birthday and remained positive. I could sense Rajiv's sadness of going through a cancer journey with me again after losing both his parents to this dreadful disease. Remembering the legacy of our special relationship, he became even more determined to make this trip happen. I was extremely delighted when Mr Al – Bahrani gave me permission to travel, insisting that I use this time to get myself even fitter for surgery.

Rajiv, my personal trainer for the week had a motto of 'no pain no gain' and he positively revelled in his new status. Every evening we debriefed on this gruelling 'survival of the fittest' plan assessing the day's effort, ending in outbursts of tearful laughter. How do you know the limit of anything? Only when you have exceeded it. Be the best as I pushed even harder than ever before – walking, running, climbing, swimming and planned work outs – passers-by on the undulating roads, all clapping and cheering my determination. Here I was feeling great and asymptomatic but living with untreated cancer plagued me with doubts about my life which was now in the cruel hands of destiny.

I stood in awe before the mountains of Madeira whose majesty marked the zenith of nature's greatness and wept at Pico D' Areiro the island's third highest peak at 1800 metres. Though my tears could not extinguish the raging flames of what could be my bleak future, they became the soothing balm for my searing pain. Climbing one peak after another became necessary for me, for it took me higher and made me stronger. I was growing in strength through these times of suffering, and every time I stumbled on the hard rocks, I learnt to walk with a gentle stride. In this way, I gathered speed and the tough climb taught me to be triumphant. Sometimes I felt as if I was on the verge of plummeting to those valleys and gorges which I could clearly see from the summit. Or I could gently soar into the high sunlit clouds across a beautiful blue sky taking a glimpse of the greatness of life. The serene mountains spread the salve of soothing air and succour to my lungs, as I savoured the breath of life.

Evenings at the Enotel Lido were filled with rapturous laughter until past midnight. Dancing, singing, drinking Maracuja and special creamy hot chocolate late into the night honoured a day well spent. Dining was a ritual savoured with the knowledge that a sumptuous three course meal would soon become a thing of the past for me. We played a strange card game 'O hell', based on the law of diminishing numbers. One could be a winner by losing everything and a thought crossed my mind, that I too could strategically win my life back by losing my growing cancer.

It was great to be MAD in MADeira. Walking on the Levada along the tunnels, we had to use light from our mobile phones to navigate our way through the darkness. Hard rocks protruded from the side walls and the low ceiling, which resulted in howling pain when each head met the rock. We were certainly not in a hard rock café, but we were hard rock follies. Travelling through this tunnel, we formed the one and only screaming musical Madeira head bangers' club with a distinct style. There was light at the end of the tunnel, and it wasn't a train coming towards us! We just needed to keep moving forward overcoming the obstacles until we were out in the brightness of the day.

One evening, torrential rain beat fiercely on our windows from which we could see the wild stormy sea. Waves unleashed their anger, smashing against the perimeter walls of our hotel. Pradip wanted to run to the sea front to experience this rage of nature but I held him back, fearing the unknown. We could see two people venturing out from a neighbouring hotel towards the edge where the water gushed fiercely, spreading and receding just as quickly. In a blink of an eye, they were over the safety barriers trying to capture this spectacle on their mobile phones. Suddenly, we lost sight of them, and discovered the next morning that one man was swept away, and the other had clamoured back to safety. The feisty sea, unruly and unforgiving, with its indomitable wrath, had claimed a soul and a serenade of grief filled the air. Here I was fighting for my life against cancer, and I failed to understand why those selfie lovers and thrill seekers were tempting fate.

This unfortunate event intensified my enquiry not just about life and death, which is inevitable for all of us, but I did welcome death of disease, death of limitations, death of ill health and death of cancer. These thoughts ebbed and flowed into my consciousness increasing my will to survive. During this time, I learnt to appreciate the value of every breath, every moment, every waking, every meal, every relationship, every walk, every sunrise and every sunset, missing nothing.

Looking out of the window of our plane in glaring sunshine, we bid farewell to this magnificent garden island taking memories of its colourful orchids and the birds of paradise, opulent in their orange colour, symbolising freedom and joy. I knew then that my past was a distant country and I was travelling to a new horizon.

The preoperative assessment was scheduled in a week before surgery just when I had secretly hoped all this would 'go away'. "It will" assured my husband, "they will be doing curative surgery". But what if they do not go ahead with surgery? "That will not happen".

We held on to each other and I knew that he was speaking from a very convincing insight.

Yes, we are still living in the void, clinging to the past and we must emerge from it. We are brave warriors and courage above everything is our finest quality. Success or failure can be neither final nor fatal. Our loved ones stand by us giving strength, but where does the courage from?

Madeira: Joy of getting fit

Mountain solace

Top of our world

One step at a time

Precious moment

TWELVE

My life in their hands

*Life is not always a matter of holding
good cards but sometimes playing a poor hand well*
- **Robert Louis Stevenson**

The preoperative assessment started early seeking the blessings of my loving mother and our revered master Sai Baba bringing an assuring energy that would sustain me through this longest day.

Waiting rooms are the same in hospitals all over the world. The bland walls of the small room were covered with the odd reprints of landscapes that no one remembers. The blue chairs on a monotonous grey carpet and an occasional table spread with well-thumbed out of date magazines welcomed us. Like others, we sat and gazed into this space in an acquiescent manner seeing people intermittently tapping their knee and looking at their watches. I was left yet again to dwell reluctantly on my oscillating waves of boredom and anxiety.

Upon hearing my name, we joined the race around the hospital for blood tests and meetings with doctors, nurses, anaesthetist, dietician and pharmacist. During one of these meetings, and to my surprise, my GP called me on my mobile to inform me that I was to take oral iron immediately. The dietician gave me a course of high protein, fish-based nutrients recommended by Mr Al-Bahrani to be taken a few days before my surgery. The anaesthetist was waiting for us and greeted us with a smile betraying a subtle sense of humour. He did not feel the need to go through all the complications that could arise from an extensive surgery. "The chances of you crossing the road and being hit by a car are higher than all the possible complications that could kill you!" I could see he loved his profession to such an extent it put us at great ease, and he connected with us as if we were close friends.

Mother's Day 10 March 2018 could not have been more significant, as I needed her by my side. The date of surgery 19 March was fast approaching as this emotional, physical and mental roller coaster gathered speed. I endeavoured to manage the barrage of stress, knowing that our state of mind influences the rate of recovery and healing of wounds. Moreover, the switching on and off of genes which produce proteins required for wound healing are known to be affected by immense emotional stress. The final blood grouping test was completed three days before surgery. My GP called to assure me that I had one of the best surgeons who had the necessary skills and I was very fortunate to be offered this option as not every clinician wants to undertake this type of surgical procedure.

The night before the D-day, I spoke to God in a way like many others before me knowing that my life was hanging in a balance. Upon hearing my plea, I heard a reassuring whisper that His plans for me were yet to unfold, and I felt a comforting hand softly wiping my tears. I lit a candle calling all our great ancestors whose timeless love spoke in my blood. "Be still and listen carefully my child for you are the epitome of the love of thousands."

This morning brought a strange calm within me. It wasn't dreary like the last few days, instead the scattering colours of sky blended into shades of blue and orange. The trees swayed in the breeze as if they were dancing to the music of time, accompanied by the melodic sound of the birds which filled the sky. Our journey to the hospital was filled with trepidation accompanied by smooth classical music and healing chants which consoled us. In our hearts these were our battle cries of hope against the legion of cancer. Songs of devotion sprang from the depths of our souls as we travelled along the highway of uncertainty, each one lost in their own thoughts.

The moment of huge significance had arrived, and without a doubt 'living in the moment' seizing the day was all that really mattered. Perhaps I had not quite understood the gravity of losing my loved ones until this day. I thought about whether or not I would see my home again, a refuge where memories of a lifetime were created. The tempestuous few months had given us little time to discuss my concerns and wishes in the event of my demise. One wish that remained in my heart which I had to convey was for Pradip to find love in his life, should I be taken away from this world and to always know that the good Lord had used us for His purpose, even though it may not be obvious to us. To thank Him for the journey we have had together, for the trials and tribulations, for without those we would not experience His blessings along the way.

We walked up three flights of stairs to the theatre area relieved that I was fit for this day. Each step reminded me of my climb on a pilgrimage in India many years ago, which came to fruition as I reached the summit of a temple, as many have done before me.

In a crowded room, the surgical team went through the procedures again and all the complications including death which was a real possibility. I saw my mother trying to hold back her tears as they trickled down her face conveying her secret that only the good Lord would understand. Tears of a mother who lost one son from a sudden heart attack, another from advanced cancer and now appealing to the Divine to save her only remaining child. She spoke a wise tale of both hope and sorrow. I assured her in the face of adversity that I would be fine. She looked up at Mr Al-Bahrani and asked, 'Is this curative surgery?', to which he put his comforting hand on her shoulder and said, "I would not do this otherwise'. We parted with a hope that we would see each other again as I received this affirmation from Pradip "See you soon, you are not going anywhere". My mother's last words to me before I was taken away were "You ARE coming back". With that farewell, which could have been my last, I was prepared to face what was coming without a blink as I embraced the power of infinity. Being in darkness did not mean that the light had disappeared. I felt that it had merely shifted to a different dimension and if I earnestly looked for it, it would have to return. As they wheeled me away, my mother asked me to recite the universal Gayatri mantra (a syllable in Sanskrit) which invokes the light from within and illuminates the mind to dispel negative energy fields, thereby protecting the vital life force. In this cultural anchor, I became prepared for my next ordeal.

I asked the anaesthetist if I could place a small picture of my guru Sai Baba under my pillow. He wondered if it was like a prayer and when I acknowledged this, he said "You will need it". Just before I was anaesthetised, I knew that I would sleep either for nine hours or for eternity where there was a place called heaven. My prayers were that God would always protect my mother and my husband whatever happened. Dying did not scare me and there was no need to blame anyone especially God for this greatest trial in my life. My family were asked to go home and wait. Their gruelling journey home was interrupted with emotions spilling into uncontrollable crying. My mother gathered herself, took charge and demanded that my husband stop the car until he was suitably calm enough to drive. She repeated that "as it is now in the lap of the gods, Daksha must fight for her life".

Several hours later, the surgeon called to inform them that everything had gone according to plan with minimum blood loss, even though the surgery was as complex and extensive as expected. He reiterated that these were still early days. When Pradip mentioned that they had been praying continuously, Mr Al-Bahrani conveyed that so did the surgical team. These words will stay with us forever.

Life can be changeable like the weather, sometimes stormy, then generous like the monsoon. Occasionally brutal as a tornado, which steals away our hopes, but also returns abundantly. Learning to love means discovering beauty in the changing seasons of life, because we are at one with the universe.

We are not human beings
having a spiritual
experience, we are spiritual
beings having a human
experience.

-Teilhard de Chardin

Source: Greatest Inspirational Quotes:
365 Days to More Happiness, Success, and Motivation by Dr Joe Tichio, 2012

THIRTEEN

In the cradle of care

Experience is not what happens to you. It's what you do with what happens to you
- Aldous Huxley

Strapped into my glider I felt the tug of the tow down the airfield as the biplane lifted me above the green fields into the sky. I felt beautifully quiet when the tow rope was released at around two thousand feet. Rising thermals continued to carry me upwards in ever increasing circles from one cloud to another. Words from the famous song "In the windmills of your mind" flowed into my heart "Like a circle in a spiral, like a wheel within a wheel, never ending nor beginning, On an ever-spinning reel… As the images unwind, Like the circles that you find, In the windmills of your mind…"

I was ascending to a place which was home only for the high soaring bird, the eagle that dominates the sky. Like my glider plane it uses its wings to glide in upward moving air, but it seems that he is stronger and more agile than my glider. Here I was flying engineless catching a glimpse of the horizon through cumulus clouds, the warm rays of the glowing sun penetrating my whole being through the canopy. I was travelling across the sky, my glider taking me to a place strangely familiar to me. The birds in a formation became my companions leading the way spreading their wings as broad as my glider and I knew we were in a time - space continuum where freedom from all limitations prevailed. A large sandstone rock formation became visible as I began to lose height. I circled round for what seemed like a long time, struck by the beauty of the changing colours from shades of brown, orange and glowing red on this rock as my orbit continued into the fine sunset. I was coming close to an inselberg or an island mountain, the ground was fast approaching and I reduced the lift but could not prevent a bumpy landing upon the base of one of the most sacred sites, Uluru (Ayer's rock) which means Great Pebble, for the aboriginal people in Central Australia. In this ancient landscape I could hear faint chants from the spirits of the ancestors.

"Wake up, wake up!" commanded my brain as if sleeping any longer from the anaesthesia might defer my conscious awareness that I am still alive. I was gasping for breath in the intensive care unit (ICU), while choking trying to reach for the call button when a doctor rushed over seeing me in distress and removed the intubation tube from my throat.

I had never realised that pain was indeed a messenger of life. I was in severe pain, had two chest drains, a catheter, oxygen mask, drips and all wired up to flashing and bleeping monitors. I felt thoroughly ravaged though morphine and other medications brought some relief. With a deep sense of emptiness inside me, my tears flowed incessantly, the stabbing pain continuously striking my diaphragm, ribs and chest wall.

Through my half open drowsy eyes, I saw my mum stroking my forehead, her soft hand resting gently on my chest and Pradip right beside her. Though they were shocked to see me in this state, they told me that the surgery was over and to be strong. The next day I was put into a chair to start moving my legs which gave me a better sense of where I was. On the third day in ICU the surgeon appeared with a smile on his face, waving a piece of paper as if I had won a Nobel prize! Not wanting to receive any bad news, I pulled the bedsheets over my face and with a hoarse voice, I requested him to get my mum and Pradip from the waiting room. He confirmed that whilst he had removed the oesophagus as planned, he decided to remove thirty-nine uninvolved lymph nodes to minimise the risk of metastases. No further treatment was required at this stage. My mother cried with relief, hugged the big man and thanked him for saving her daughter's life. In terms of complications, we had to wait until I was out of intensive care.

Waking up from a drug induced sleep, I would see a kaleidoscopic set of characters around me, each armed with their particular brand of test kits. They probed, prodded, injected and talked with great enthusiasm, as if from a well- rehearsed script. It was like being a patient in a drama, who was not able to protest at anything being done to them. My throat was dry and deeply sore, my oxygen mask steamed up, and the various pieces of equipment plugged into me, created a cacophony of noise which astounded me. I felt like an advanced version of resuscitation Annie, a mannikin used in first aid and medical training. Doctors struggled with frustration to locate those veins for a canula, and I felt like I was being harpooned. Even blood sucking bats might have been more merciful.

The next few days proved to be even more challenging as being bed ridden in intensive care was not pleasant. One fine day, the hospital chaplain, a lovely Irish lady came by and said in an ecclesiastical voice "I've come to pray for you". Startled, as bad news is not usually given with such a smile, but I still had my doubts, I asked her 'Am I going to die?' "Good grief, no, the whole team's doing their absolute best to make sure that does not happen".

A few days later, I was so frightened to be isolated to a solitary room in a ward, waiting anxiously for my family to come. Feeling groggy from morphine, having nausea and suffering from frequent dumping (rapid gastric emptying accompanied by severe abdominal cramps) worried me that I would have to live with this for ever. Excruciating pain was a constant reminder of the site where the surgeon's knife had done its damndest. Having a fixed nasal feeding tube into the throat and to the stomach made me feel like the victim of a horrid biochemical attack. "Have I been reduced to this level of embarrassing dependency?" I still had a catheter and a bed pan, and I was truly humbled by the care from the nurses looking after me. They do such thankless tasks with compassion and dedication. Knowing the high risk of deterioration after this type of surgery they were monitoring me with utmost care.

The MDT would make their regular ward rounds and being heavily sedated, I was unaware of their whispered discussions. Often during the night, I would wake up with tormenting pain and haunting thoughts about losing my life against cancer just as my twin brother had. Sometimes I would hallucinate seeing people in the room who were not there, so my morphine dose was reduced but my sleep medication made me feel much worse in the mornings. It was like being in a life raft tossed about by colossal waves in a storm suffering the wrath of Poseidon.

It was apparent that the hospital was understaffed with only a few nurses skilled to deliver intravenous medication. My sugar levels soared, ketones appeared in my urine, metformin was not working and out of desperation, I requested insulin. Unfortunately, as I had to wait until the morning rounds, my nights were horrendous wishing I could just sleep my way through them. I knew I had to take more control lest I had post-surgical complications together with the possible damaging effects of high sugar levels.

Many patients in my new ward remained passive even though their screaming conveyed their discomfort. Each new day became an episode from a hospital television series, where I became an observer amazed by the theatrics of unique personalities providing light-hearted entertainment, a welcome distraction from the pain which had arrived in my life like an unwanted gift.

I was so glad to see a bowl of warm soup in front of me, but I hesitated, aware that I no longer had a food pipe. My stomach had been stretched into a long tube in my chest and the fear of not being able to swallow paralysed me. I was about to take a sip, when the doctors rushed in with great concern instructing me to stop immediately. I had an anastomosis leak, leading to pneumonia and I was rushed for an X-Ray, followed by infusion of antibiotics for several days. I remained nil by mouth with a nasal feed through a tube into my restructured stomach that continuously and painfully pulled my nose. I was back in a critical condition and my husband was assured by a kind and considerate sister in charge that though I was in danger, the best option was a slow conservative approach to deal with the leak and the lung infection. It was like being inebriated without the option not to drink! I kept telling myself that the pain I feel everyday would become my strength for the next day.

During my hospital stay, I must have spent around 36,000 minutes reflecting on my whole life, of which it took three decades of searching only to realise that the holy spirit dwelt in me as me. That faith was the very breath of victory and when we are truly awakened to this reality, we begin to make the right choices in this life of purpose. But before we are able to do that, we need to atone for the differences that we harboured with our nearest and dearest. I thought deeply about the loss of my father and both my brothers and realised how precious time had passed away like sand through the hour glass. Every night I slept thereafter in gratitude remembering what God has taught me that I never need to worry about tomorrow. I survived yesterday. I am alive and dealing with today. With His help, I can face tomorrow and whatever may come my way.

In the carousel of care, we experience a world we had not known before. We sail through the sea of despair as well as hope, at times our lives overlapping with others. We laugh and learn as we share our woes and all that remains with us is a memory. The moment passes with sunshine or a cloudy day, but a new chance, a new life or a new beginning descends from the heavens. And the greatest love of all makes its home in us.

The day after

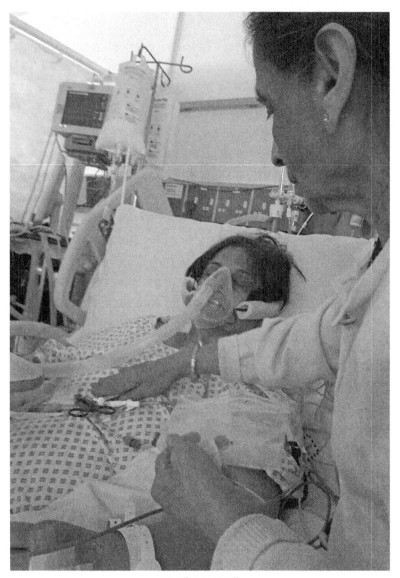

ICU "I see You"

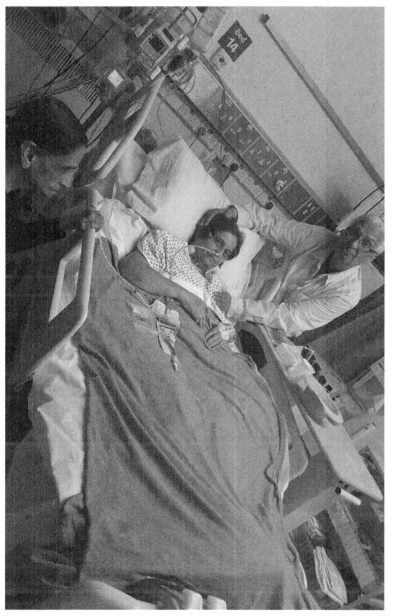

ICU Awakening

FOURTEEN

The waiting game

Patience is just not the ability to wait; it's about our demeanour while waiting

We all have learnt to wait for one reason or another. If you wait for a bus and miss it, another one will come along or you can choose to walk or take a taxi. But waiting for treatment in hospital, scans, medicines, physiotherapy, ward rounds, nursing and personal care, happens in its own time. Every day you are waiting anxiously to hear how you are recovering from major surgery. It becomes a new life, with helpless dependency on other people, making you feel alone and remote, when most of your life you have been self-sufficient. The maxim 'Carpe diem' empowered me after one torrential night of falling tears splashing against the windows of my heart caged with consternation.

 'Healing through sleep', a guided meditation rescued me from my restless nights and I no longer needed sleep medication. When receiving blood transfusion, I lay awake in the dark hours chanting the universal gayatri mantra increasing the positive vibrations around me.

At times when I was overwhelmed with painful emotions, my mother would narrate those inspiring stories from the Hindu epic Ramayana – where Rama is the personification of all goodness conquering forces of negativity. I would hear her soft voice teaching me "Om Anna Purnaye Namah - My body and spirit are nourished with Divine Energy". I would wake up refreshed but not being able to keep my eyes focused on the pages of a book, I listened to audio books which took me to faraway places.

Some evenings from my window, I could see the bright lights above the Watford Football Club stadium on Vicarage Road and hear the chanting of their theme song 'I'm still standing better than I ever did' which had a special meaning for me. The sights, smells and sounds of the hospital ward were difficult to ignore with its own blend of 'fragrance' – antiseptic and bleachy. Powdery blue coloured walls with faded pictures had scuff marks revealing thousands of trolley bumps. In this rather abrasive atmosphere, I could just imagine Judy Garland singing

"Clang, clang, clang" went the trolley

"Ding, ding, ding" went the bell

"Zing, zing, zing" went my heartstrings

For the moment I saw him (*the surgeon*) I fell in a spell, in anticipation of the news he might be bringing.

Unable to leave my bed, some patients would come to me, and share their personal stories, which made me realise how we were all connected through our suffering along this difficult road. They would look forward to family visits which brought temporary relief, but no one could understand the emptiness they felt. A kind lady next to me had gastroenteral surgery and her well educated daughters would discuss her discharge plans. She became quite distressed at the prospect of being sent to a care home apparently without her consent. She sought my advice and I conveyed that she might be eligible for home care. Taking control of her own life, and being more assertive with her family, she returned home happily.

Another patient, at age 16 during the second world war was with the ambulance service during the blitz. She re-lived her traumatic experiences of the war, pulling people out of burning buildings and often finding dead bodies. She got up one night and started shouting and screaming to get everyone out of the building. I calmed her back to sleep reassuring her that everyone was safe and sound. I learnt that the same pain medication can affect people in very different ways.

Engaging with other people's pain and helping in small ways during my critical condition took me away from my own suffering. Going beyond myself to help others, I realised that these strange moments were part of my own recovery. When they left the hospital, their appreciative smile conveyed that I still had a purpose for my extended stay, not realising how important they had been in my own healing! Many patients were discharged before me which made me feel like an orphan waiting for a loving family to come and take me home.

Outside the ICU, my mother and my husband met a couple distraught because their daughter was in an extremely critical condition and the doctors had given them the worst outcome. The lady cried

"I don't want to lose my only daughter. She has been my best friend throughout my life". Hearing this, my mother comforted her, understanding her pain. My husband consoled her with 'have hope and faith, miracles do happen'. Forces beyond medicine are known to help through positive thoughts. He suggested she continued to talk to her daughter who was in a coma, and to draw her through her positive loving messages. We knew of many instances where people have come out of coma and upon regaining consciousness have recalled the messages they had 'heard'.

I had constant breast pain, as a result of radical surgery, and I needed new undergarments with the required support due to my changed body shape. My husband and my mother embarked on the hunt for these whilst I was in hospital. Suitably embarrassed, Pradip would put my mother forward to explain my needs in case a man hanging around women's lingerie department would raise eyebrows and alert security. My mother had to go up and down the stairs, lifts and escalators despite her heart condition with the determination to help me get the 'support' I needed. They made numerous journeys to many Marks and Spencer's stores and their returns policy was greatly appreciated. Eventually when my new undergarments did fit me, I cried and laughed at the same time feeling as if I had been awarded a special prize! Such amusing moments were delightful distractions from my nagging pain and from then on, I welcomed the ward rounds with a rejuvenated confidence rather than dread.

For the first time, I noticed a tall well-dressed lady with bright blue eyes and a beaming smile, walking in front of her husband dressed in his hospital gown. He would lean on her with both his hands as she led him up and down the ward corridor in tandem several times a day. They reminded me of a popular song 'A bicycle made for two'. I learnt later that he had had a near death experience and his ability to walk was critical to his recovery. Even when the physiotherapists did not come, I was greatly encouraged by them to continue walking to improve my lung function after its collapse during surgery. Thereafter, mum would carefully disconnect me from all equipment and, take me for walks, steering the IV drip stand. We would come across the now famous 'bicycle made for two' and our unspoken exchanges relayed 'Catch me if you can'. This became our race round the corridors with our own version of chariots of fire. Vangelis's evocative theme echoed as we hastened our steps 'walking with hopes in our hearts and wings at our heels, and when I walked, I felt God's Presence'. On the day I was discharged, I wished them God speed.

The only way we can be break the chains of pain and isolation is when we know that there is someone alone facing more adversity than us. If only, we reach out and touch another to alleviate their suffering.

I am here

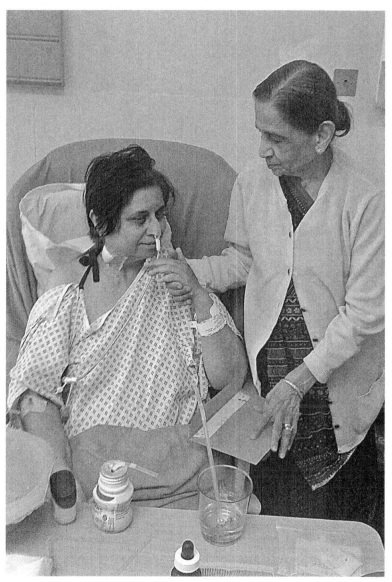

Problems with a naso-gastric tube

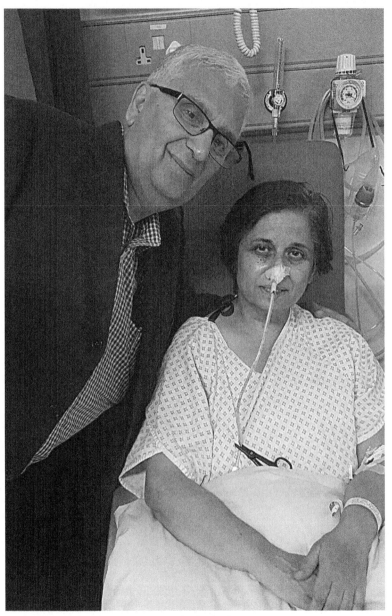

How do we look?

FIFTEEN

Everybody needs somebody

Where there is love there is life

- Mahatma Gandhi[14]

God does have a sense of humour and also loves to attend parties. There was at Easter, a parade of young volunteers who were distributing Easter eggs to patients in hospital. It seemed rather ironic that here I was nil by mouth just savouring in my imagination the taste of chocolate!

Unexpected visits from my friends greatly surprised me and were like pennies from heaven. Naturally I did not wish anyone to see me in this state, but when they made me laugh, my nasal tube would bounce up and down in rhythm with my abdomen bemusing everyone who had the privilege of hearing my bizarre rhapsody. Strangely, none of them appeared to be shocked as I expected but were amazed at my rather favourable demeanour. In their presence, I felt like one who had performed a trapeze triple somersault in a circus and then walked the Niagara gorge on a tight rope as the famous Blondin did in 1859.

The medical team had conveyed to me that I was their star patient, and according to them everything was going to plan, despite some adversities. With all the acrobatics I had to perform, I neither fell

_____

[14] Courtesy www.mkgandhi.org

from the trapeze act nor from the tightrope, though sometimes I swayed a bit which made everybody gasp. Little did I know that I wasn't alone walking the tightrope across a thunderous waterfall below, but I was being carried safely across to the other side by an embodiment of energy without the fear of falling.

The carnival of friends had come to town with bells, whistles and balloons, all cheering and clapping, making me forget the gravity of what I had been through. These angelic clowns showed me that life is one big extravaganza, with moments that both terrify us and also bring magical experiences. As a child I remembered that a day would come for the circus to pack up and leave for pasture's new and soon it would be my turn to pack and go home.

The Madeira head bangers, Rajiv and Priti made frequent visits, pulling an Easter bunny out of the hat which was aptly named 'Cutie from Cambridge', and my mascot stayed with me ever after. I was woken up with the words "Allo Allo…what are you doing lying down? I hope you have a reasonable excuse for this?" Jenny A and Steve, an ex-policeman frog marched me to the hospital entrance, where for the first time I saw life beyond the hospital. The laughing policeman didn't have to cuff me as I was already chained to the drip stand!

I felt a soothing breeze come in to calm my inner storm as I heard the soft sounds of the Hanuman Chalisa, a Sanskrit hymn which fills one with the vibrational energy to ward off adversity, suffering and pain. It has been credited to a 16th-century poet Tulsidas in Awadhi, an Indo-Aryan language which originates from northern

India. This meditative practice of reciting mantras can help to still the mind, experience deep awareness and allow our body, mind and spirit to relax.

Our dear friends Mahesh, Amit and Michele gathered by my hospital bedside and were warmly surprised to see me in a far better state than expected. They had taken it upon themselves to chant daily this sacred hymn throughout my ordeal to keep me safe from negative energies. It comes from the great Indian epic Ramayana in which Hanuman, the monkey God is endowed with the divine strength for overcoming adversity. My mother always engaged in this legend from Hindu mythology where Hanuman, a great devotee of Lord Rama, displayed such intelligence and prowess to overcome all obstacles. He had fought the armies of Ravana, the demon king of Lanka and emerged victorious. It is believed that he was destined to remain on the earthly plane for the protection of mankind. Interestingly, upon reflection it happened to be the 14th December when my tumour was initially identified, which also is observed and celebrated unofficially as an international 'monkey day' and 'all things simian'.

Sister Pavalam, also known by her friends as the medicine woman, with her enchanting smile continued vibrionic healing, sharing with me many success stories. Chhaya gave me Reiki and reflexology, gently massaging my painful body which relieved my symptoms to a great extent. Her children Jay and Vibhuti with their laughing eyes and a wry sense of humour would tickle me as they commented about my party dress (hospital gown) conjuring up cakes for my husband's birthday. Whilst my dear mother had spent her 87th birthday a few days earlier in intensive care, clasping my hand, Pradip's birthday brought new tidings with merriment in the air, as preparations were being made for my discharge.

Terry, an old friend from our village, upon arriving from Egypt came directly to the hospital. She had been severely challenged watching her husband die from this cruel disease and seeing me survive all the hardships, she had an unexpected resurgence of a lost faith.

Those few days brought extraordinary transformation, making me realise that every person and every moment is valuable, taking nothing for granted. Would this be my moment of change? Because, it is just not enough to acknowledge special days, but far more important to convey what is nestled in our hearts. Unspoken words cannot go anywhere until they are received by the person we love. Everything perishes except love which is immortal. This was

my awakening. I had often requested hospital radio to play Louis Armstrong's "What a Wonderful World" for all the noble souls who were making life possible.

Despite being constantly dehydrated and unable to eat and drink satisfactorily, I still managed to pass the swallow test. The long nasal tube was removed by cutting the stiches in the nose, akin to an umbilical cord cut from the mother's womb, releasing a piercing shriek that cut through the silence of the ward.

The hospital provided me with a starter pack of medication, energy drinks and literature on food management. I still had several dressings at the surgery sites and chest drains with little advice on how to deal with them. There was little information and guidance provided on what was expected of my caring loved ones. Preparing to leave was an ordeal. I still had raw wounds, needed a walking stick and had difficulty getting into the car. I felt bitterly cold even on this bright spring day and as we went over each bump in the road, I let out a scream with the whole of my body, my fingers clinging on to the cushions that supported me.

Homeward bound, from the window of the car I saw a bright new world not known to me and my heart could hear the rhythm of life that spoke of freedom beyond measure. In the depths of my soul, I knew then that the forces of darkness were left confused and lost as it was not their day. This was the first day of my new life.

Our struggles become a source of strength for us and for others. Through suffering, we soften our way to restoration. Let us not underestimate the power of love.

The tight rope by Daksha Trivedi

A matter of trust

Belief and Trust

A person started walking on a rope that was tied between two tall towers. He walked slowly balancing a long stick in his hands and with his son sitting on his shoulders.

The people in his surrounds stood watching him with bated breath. They were very anxious about his safety. When the man slowly reached the second tower every one clapped, whistled and welcomed him. They shook hands with him and even took selfies.

The man then asked the crowd "Do you all think I can walk back on the same rope now from this side to that side?" The entire crowd shouted in one voice "Yes, Yes, you can" "Do you trust me?", he asked. They responded in unison, "Yes, yes, we are ready to bet on you".

To this response, the man asked, "Okay then, can any one of you sit on my shoulder? I will take you to the other side safely"

There was stunned silence. Everyone became quiet.

Belief is different. Trust is different. For Trust you need total surrender.

We believe in God. But do we trust Him?

-Anonymous

SIXTEEN

The home coming

It's a strange feeling coming home. Everything is the same as it ever was. What has really changed is you.

Entering our village from the High Street I saw our black and white mock Tudor house with georgian windows. Our car gently rolled onto the cobbled drive cluttered with fallen leaves rain soaked in dark brown and orange. I smiled at the mysterious laughing buddha in the porch, as my mother went round the back and opened the large oak front door. I entered the house, with an unsteady gait and leaning heavily on my walking stick. My mother was holding a candle placed in the centre of a decorative plate filled with rose petals. To touch her feet in reverence was my desire but alas I could not bend down, and we both cried as she spread the light from the flame over me by the gentle wave of her hand. The memory of leaving home, twenty-five days earlier, not knowing if I was ever to return came flooding back. Strange was the providence that brought me back from the brink of disaster.

It was early evening and I was in so much pain, feeling tired, dehydrated and sick. Supported by cushions, I sat down in an upright chair thinking that this was the beginning of a whole new way of life. I could not consume anything, except small amounts of Ensure, a nutritious high protein but tasteless drink and I suffered from regular 'dumping', as a result of surgery and the way the food is processed in my new system. I had to sleep at 30 degrees to prevent any reflux given that my stomach was a long tube that started so high up in my chest. With great difficulty we managed to go up the stairs slowly and use several hard pillows to prop me at the required angle to make me comfortable. Thus, began a 24- hour vigil on me. The nights were particularly difficult for everyone and I cried with pain, as I was incapacitated in so many ways. My mind was inundated with so many questions "Will I be able to sleep? Will I be able to swallow, eat, drink, walk? Will my lungs improve? How long would I have to suffer this?" My emotions ricocheted between highs and lows and I prayed that whatever I had to endure be bearable, as I saw my family suffer with me. I overheard my mother praying "Dear Lord, please give me all the pain that is upon my daughter and free her from suffering". With anger, I demanded a retraction and a promise from her never to make a request like that again, explaining to her that each one of us has to follow our destiny.

Being a vegetarian, it was difficult to know the types of food my newly repaired body could tolerate. We had to become creative in terms of nature, density and portions, and which foods would absorb and digest well. "I don't want to eat" became my daily mantra having lost the appetite and the taste for food. Morphine gave me low moods, accompanied by nausea. My mother persisted on making me eat like a baby, little more often, and with remarkable alacrity, she tried anything and everything from her vast knowledge of recipes that would strengthen me. Often, she would request Pradip to identify the type of nourishing foods from other nutritional and medical centres, that would cater for not only a post oesophagectomy patient but also a vegetarian which made it more difficult. Regaining and maintaining weight was a constant source of concern. She would regularly grind different breakfast cereal mixes to add to various dishes hoping that I might be able to consume small amounts. The fear of choking and swallowing difficulties arising as a result of eating prevented me from wanting to try anything. Knowing that nausea and sickness occurred regularly after food intake further compounded the problem. We had to follow the process of trial and error of many different foods, drinks and frequency of eating to overcome these hurdles alongside pain management after surgery. It came as a revelation that there was no standard dietary regime as every individual's body system reacts differently to the same foods with varying tolerance levels.

Serendipity had connected me with Michelle, whom I had never met before. I learnt that her mother was suffering from severe oesophagitis and was having to manage food and drink intake with regular widening of her inflamed food pipe. This was the first time I was able to talk to somebody who had similar challenges and looking at her quality of life despite these ongoing difficulties, hope crystallised in my heart and we did not remain strangers for long.

This was absolutely a road less travelled as no one had prepared us for what to expect after discharge. We felt there was a huge focus on treatment and not enough emphasis on support through this recovery process. It took a lot of tenacity and ingenuity to put the necessary components together to meet my basic needs. We managed to get an electric bed and a recliner chair to help me sit and sleep properly. With great reluctance, I had to accept that I was and will be functioning differently than before. Excessive dumping, followed by sweating and nausea, was extremely frightening as my weight continued to decline making me weaker. I would become breathless at the slightest exertion, accompanied by the fear of falling as my blood sugar levels dropped. We felt we were on our own, except for my GP, with little or no support to take us through this onerous process.

When I saw my GP the first time after surgery, her face conveyed deep relief as she said, "I am so happy to see you come through these doors". I walked in breathless, using a walking stick, and I knew straightaway that I was in the care of someone to whom I owe so much for without her professional intuition I may not be alive to write this testimony. She explained honestly that given I was the first case of this kind in her practice in several years, and her not being an expert in this field, she would do her utmost to provide the necessary care for my symptoms.

Despair began to dissolve, and determination took its place as I became increasingly proactive in my recovery programme. I liaised with the hospital dietician to resolve my dietary problems and I continued with my post-surgery physical training programme with the exercise referral coordinator. Walking daily became mandatory for improving my lung function as my survival depended on it. It started with walking round my house and in our beautiful courtyard, gradually venturing out into the village, creating milestones – the bakery, the post office, the nursing home and then beyond. Jenny G had taught me to overcome any uneasiness about people asking how I was, and I became free from my fears of how I was perceived, accepting their encouraging words. The use of my walking stick became less frequent, and the day I cast it aside, I felt liberated.

My lungs responded and I could feel the power of breathing, like a first engine cough of a vintage propeller airplane which then runs smoothly to a gentle sound of So..hum So..hum breathing. My mother described this moment like a baby taking its first breath after a smack on the bottom, which releases a cry of happiness. Pradip continued to research on care after an esophagectomy. It seemed as if I was doing far better than expected and a day would come when we would look back and know that this ordeal was a small price to pay for a gift of life. However, he never revealed to me the harsh reality of what could go wrong, even at this stage, including my prognosis and survival. He internalised so much that I discovered months later that it had a silent impact on him, and he could not talk to anyone about this. His demeanour was akin to the Battle of Britain fighter pilots who went out on a mission and when they came home, they would be slumped in a sofa either sleeping or pretending to be reading, exhausted but also in a high state of readiness for the next mission.

We travel together because we are bound by the same path.
Home is where our heart belongs, indelible in the infinite space
of sacredness. Do we really love enough to make a difference?

After discharge and during recovery

Home again – few days post discharge

With Mr Al-Bahrani -Ten days post discharge

At six months - Didn't we do well?

Lean on me

To my dear mother
We share the same heartbeat

She came to conquer my fears
And ease my suffering
Her presence washing away my tears
Though her own heart aching
Yes, we share the same heart- beat...

Her faith unwavering, her patience unending
Holding the power to make everything work out
Every moment coaxing and calming
Never complaining of a burnout
Yes, we share the same heart- beat...

She became my heaven on earth
Through her life burdened with pain
She gave me a new birth
My journey was not in vain
Yes, we share the same heart- beat...

Her selfless love and giving
Sprung hope in my heart
Making my life worth living
Never to be apart
Yes, we share the same heartbeat...

How can I thank you mother?
My angel of hopes and dreams
I know there is none other
Than your love pouring in a stream
Yes, we share the same heartbeat...

-Daksha Trivedi

SEVENTEEN

Who cares for carers?

Doctors diagnose, surgeons operate, nurses heal,
and caregivers make sense of it all
– Brett H. Lewis[15]

There is no time to think what you can or cannot cope with when you are faced with helping your loved ones go through an unexpected cancer journey.

My husband had not only supported me through my twin brother's cancer journey but also kept a brave face for my mother throughout her journey of losing her loved ones. Now he had to deal with the uncertainty of my diagnosis ensuring that I would always face the sun without dwelling on the shadows of despair. Despite sharing the same uncertainty, Pradip would make everything feel okay. It was only during my recovery phase that I realised what he was going through, and this caused me much heartache though he was unable to talk about his feelings.

Carer burden can be as insidious as the cancer, thriving on one's vulnerability. Walking through my cancer journey without knowing where or how to access support has taken a toll on my husband's health.

---

[15] Source: Family Caregiving: A Step-by-Step Guide to Successful Caregiving by Brett H. Lewis, 2012

We only had the one consultation when I was given the diagnosis and during the following three months as well as post-surgery he was on an overdrive with little or no dialogue with medical teams about coping with everything that was happening. The shock of it all meant he spent much time on researching the evidence around oesophageal cancer prognosis keeping the disturbing statistics to himself unable to discuss with anyone, especially me or my mother. He put a hold on his business schedule as he accompanied me to all my tests, scans and hospital visits spending much time waiting and wondering, then conveying a daily account to my mother. In his presence my mother and I felt good, reassured and courageous, not realising that he could be on a gradual melt down.

During my hospital stay, my mother and Pradip would drive three hours a day for daily visits, reaching home late at night after seeing me fall asleep so they could be assured I was pain free for that restful time. They would both wake up early, prepare their dinner and leave home around midday, spending almost seven hours by my bedside, wondering how I would be and whether or not I had improved or deteriorated, but always bringing a cheerful disposition.

My mother coped firstly through denial that my condition was serious followed by planning ahead all the items I would need in hospital which included how she would manage my food intake when I was discharged. She only had one belief that everything will be alright in its own time. The real challenge came when I was discharged, as no one was given instructions on what to expect of them to help my recovery. It was like driving a car without experience and no highway code, bouncing off the side walls and into other fairground dodgems.

It began with sleepless nights, increasing fatigue and worry as Pradip and my mother tendered to all my needs day after day, night after night. There was for Pradip, an unrecognised exponential rise in physical and mental exhaustion which resulted in moments of total silence and inability to comprehend what was being said. Emotionally he became displaced and isolated unable to free himself from the psychological impact. Gradually the pain became so intense that it altered his view of normality and he would question every decision "Have I done the right thing?"

A large UK survey of 3400 carers found that caring had a negative impact on both physical and mental health, with more than a third delaying medical treatment due to caring responsibilities[16]. Contributing factors were lack of timely and appropriate support including practical and emotional support, adding to stress and anxiety. Care giving burden is associated with negative health outcomes from this relentless stress affecting the quality of life of family carers. Several months into my recovery we began to address Pradip's extreme tiredness, energy depletion and behavioural changes. We contacted local carer organisations who were unable to respond at the time and there was very little information on professional or voluntary support that was much needed during this very difficult time. When he saw the GP, he was found to be anaemic and given that stress can result in a

---

[16] https://www.ageuk.org.uk/documents/engb/ campaigns/carers_week_2012_ in_sickness_and_in_health.pdf?dtrk=true

weakened immune system, it came as no surprise when he was diagnosed with shingles.

Gradually, as I became increasingly self-reliant, both my mother and my husband focused more on their own well-being which had been neglected due to our prevailing circumstances. We intensified our self- healing strategies and stayed constructively in mindfulness (living in the moment without judgement) through meditation, prayers, exercise and light-hearted activities, and most importantly talking together openly about what we were going through. We were becoming restored in our togetherness heedful that no one should ever feel isolated in their struggles and that despite the temporary toll on the health of our loved ones, no one was made to feel a burden. Instead we learnt to seek and gratefully accept help from well-wishers. We all became united in embracing the wellbeing of each other and determined to handle any challenge in a way that would make us grow together. We took small steps to harness our energy to regain a fine balance, joy, and hope in our lives. My mother quickly adapted to the demands of the situation and became not only a caregiver but a care manager to both Pradip and me. She relished in the challenge to show herself that she would do whatever it took to achieve the only goal at this time which was to make her family well again. In her schedule she factored in her own respite time of reading, resting and watching her favourite programmes. She even made us forget her long term condition of hypertrophic cardiomyopathy, a disease in which the heart muscle becomes abnormally thick, making it harder for the heart to pump blood, with a risk of heart failure. Her highly efficient way of working in a detached manner and being adaptable to meet all the changing needs made our lives so much more manageable. This experience has brought to the fore, the need for accessible support groups to prevent social isolation and where people can be signposted to get appropriate help before their health deteriorates. It's a great pity that the Macmillan booklets "Looking after someone with cancer", "Working while caring for someone with cancer" and " Understanding oesophageal cancer"[17] came to us so late for it would have alleviated many difficulties if we had been signposted to it early on.

My husband found the following tips particularly useful:
- Accept your feelings
- Educate yourself about your loved one's illness – making good choices
- Learn to recognise the key signs of burnout
- Keep in mind the positive aspects of care giving
- Think about coping tools- focus on what you can control and let go of what you cannot
- Take good care of yourself – exercise, diet and sleep, maintaining other interests, and self-healing that bring peace, for example meditation strategies
- Find someone you can talk to or join a support group - identify resources early, prevent social isolation, manage stress
- Set yourself goals - be realistic about what you can do and what you cannot, then ask for help

---

[17] Macmillan Cancer Support 2019; Looking after someone with cancer; Macmillan Cancer Support 2015; Working while caring for cancer; Macmillan Cancer Support 2017 Understanding oesophageal cancer

- Find about respite care and/or carer support organisations
- Talk to a professional for a range of services available such as counselling and holistic approaches to maintain good health

We can only care for others from strength rather than weakness. Carers may feel they are letting their patients down if they show themselves as distressed or fearful but being in denial of these powerful emotions can further exasperate an already difficult situation.

On this long road to healing, we need to look after ourselves so that we can be comforted in the knowledge that compassionate care is the greatest gift we can give to our loved ones. In giving such care, we discover the limitless power of love never imagined before.

EIGHTEEN

Beyond myself

*Be grateful for whoever comes because each has
been sent as a guide from beyond*
- Rumi

The newfound *me* declared with conviction that I was no longer
defined by my cancer. Nor by my fears, thoughts, emotions and
pain which I learnt over time to observe with detachment. I had
undergone a metamorphic change from my bilateral life to one
that was radial in its nature. Somewhere inside me I discovered
a spiritual warrior, who was ready to conquer this battle of life
enabling me to connect with the world in a way I had not done
before. I understood the true meaning of a little less of me and more
of the others allowing new energy to flow from my loving heart. I
was therefore able to draw vital goodness I needed not only from
people but also from my environment.

Dr Rhian Simpson and I were good friends at Cambridge where we
studied epidemiology. Even now, recalling the days gone by helped
to buffer the trauma from my surgery. Shockingly she revealed to me
that her cousin had recently died of the same oesophageal cancer
and whilst I was so fortunate to be alive, Rhian spent some time
putting into perspective the scale of my operation and how it would
impact on my life in the future. She put me on the road of planning
my whole life taking into account what has been a disproportionate
work life balance, which now had to change radically. I was not

uncomfortable with this as it brought a fresh sense of setting priorities for my renewed life that promised wholeness.

International folk dancing has been my passion for many years, where some good and understanding friends tolerate my two left feet. If I don't have to think about my condition, I can imagine myself dancing and my heart beating in time to the music which allows me to escape into a moment free of worry. Just as in life, with every step forward, there is also a step back, but here the ticking of the clock goes unnoticed. Jill and Peter Bransby from Rainmakers dance club performed an amalgamation of song and dance in our lounge and though unable to join them physically, I exulted in their performance. Sometime later they persuaded me to visit an English Heritage site called 'Wrest Park' where I was gently coaxed into walking further distances, pushing the boundaries of my ability. Time and distance were covered with great ease while we engaged in our usual intellectual banter on life, current affairs and academia, bringing nostalgic memories of our days at Cambridge. They introduced me to a new world of art which ignited the spirit of my inner child into the realm of a magical experience, truly meditative and conducive to my recovery.

A welcome distraction came in the form of the FIFA world cup 2018, which elated me to great heights. Scheduled time for games became sacrosanct and fulfilled my psychological need to escape into another world. I was absorbed by the gladiatorial games and saw the 'fight to win and survive'. Added to this, my mother's rudimentary comments on the game she did not fully understand was a great source of amusement. The whole experience encouraged a cathartic release of pain and tension. In particular, the exhilaration of Wimbledon breathed new life into me as I watched the players battle out in the scorching heat and Love-love all took on a different meaning. As the adrenaline surged inside me, it provided an anaesthetic relief and I imagined being in the front row savouring strawberries and cream. The thrill of the crowds elated me as I watched Djokovic versus Anderson and Kerber versus Williams fighting it out on the hallowed lawns, the clambering applause broken by sudden stillness with the umpire's coaxing words "Quiet please". My pain went into hiding for a short while allowing me to enjoy the game of champions. For the first time since coming home, I slept like a baby.

I felt as if I was in a train and every few days, people from my past entered my compartment and travelled some distance, reminiscing over old times which proved to be another pain relief programme.

While watching Lion King, and hearing Simba singing "It means no worries. For the rest of your days, it's our problem-free philosophy Hakuna Matata!", I drifted back to my childhood in Kenya. Scenes from the film of Masai Mara brought back past memories of circling the Mount Kilimanjaro in a six-seater Piper-Piper aircraft which landed on a rough airstrip directly into the wildlife game reserve of Masai Mara. Our pilot captain John flew us amongst the cotton wool clouds over the Rift Valley and through the lightning storms. This trip was in honour of my elder brother, Ashwin, who had unfortunately passed away suddenly at a young age, being only 45, and just a few days after we had shared poignant and beautiful memories of our special time in Kenya. We had overcome our unexplained separateness and reignited our love. We were to meet the next morning, but sadly fate had betrayed both of us. However, Simba had left a deep impression in my mind with his wise message of how we are all connected in this great circle of life. A few months later I was inspired to create a colourful impression of Simba which continues to bring me great joy.

Healing Art

Wisdom from Africa

The classroom from Pangani Girls School (formerly Duchess of Gloucester, Nairobi, Kenya) was transported from the past to the present in my living room, where a mayhem of laughter and joviality prevailed amongst my school friends. In the medical parlance this is known as "gelastic seizure or epilepsy", nevertheless it proved to be a most pleasant experience. This time though our unruly behaviour would not land us standing in the school corridor facing the wall but sitting in our sofas relishing afternoon tea. Coming together during this difficult time was certainly different and left an inimitable mark in the canvas of our hearts. Their brand of bonhomie and idiosyncratic humour was in great abundance. Little did I realise that our neighbour Sue Chapman, a local historian had spent some time in Kenya and Tanzania, and upon seeing me would greet me in fluent Swahili, bringing back the memories of a marketplace in Nairobi. I felt a little ashamed that I could not remember the language I grew up with, but in these moments, I could forget my pain for a short while.

Others who came of their own accord saw me much more from their hearts than their eyes. Ila made frequent trips from London bringing the love and care of a sister despite the challenges of organising her son's wedding. I was pleasantly surprised to be offered regular professional support by my friend Dr Ranje Sivakumar who spent many days counselling our family through this process. This emotional sedative not only tamed our minds but in the coldness of the aftermath brought a sense of balance and stability, which was most needed.

Family members visiting were expecting to see the worst but were astounded at the level of my recovery. Recounting my ordeal to them was particularly difficult for my mother as the intense pain of losing her son was still fresh in her mind. She just decided to ignore any notion of cancer but focused more on the curative surgery for aggressive polyps. My cousin Kalpna with whom I grew up, held my hand and gently walked me to the bakery only a short distance away. She challenged me that by the time of her next visit, I should be able to walk to the end of the village. 'Walking back to happiness' by Helen Shapiro hummed in my mind which became 'walking back to healthiness'. Knowing my love of literature, she later surprised me with a 1000 piece jigsaw puzzle called "Fantasy Bookshop". This absorbing brain teaser became a natural anaesthetic for all of us. My mother who had never played this game before was so enamoured that she reminisced about her childhood in Mombasa. With each colourful piece of the jigsaw she placed on the board, she was piecing together facets of her interesting life which I managed to record for posterity. With great admiration, I discovered the depth of her character full of dogged resilience to be able to put up such a fight for her daughter's life. She looked at me and I could sense by looking into her eyes that she had travelled back into her past as she narrated stories from her childhood in Kenya, her long forgotten memories jolting her mind. For the first time in my life, hearing her speak with both happiness and sorrow, we felt an exceptional bond that had remained elusive for so long. In these special moments, I recognised the wonderful truth about my dear mother and her life of sacrifice enduring all hardships. She willingly agreed for me to record the oral history of her life, and one particular incident that stands out is how she overcame fear of death during the war when air raid warning sirens were heard. She knew that her loving father would come post haste to her rescue as she hid in the underground shelters. She knew that she was safe in her father's arms.

On the wall of our dining room hangs a photograph of twenty-two girls from underprivileged backgrounds from Andhra Pradesh, India. We were honoured to sponsor and provide pastoral care at the Vydehi Institute of Nursing Sciences, Bangalore, South India as directed by Sai Baba. Upon hearing about my surgery, they collectively shared prayers of healing to reach me, their "Amma" meaning mother. A beautiful rendition of devotional healing songs from two young songbirds, Sai Pratyusha and Sai Chinmayee specially recorded for me all the way from Bangalore, filled those empty spaces in my heart, teaching me to love life again.

Our Sai family, both from the UK and abroad, shared with us many accounts of miraculous recovery of people from serious conditions. They had drawn courage and strength from the immense faith and love they carried at all times. In particular, the Sathya Sai Mobile Hospital team of doctors, Dr Narasimhan and Dr Prasad provided valuable advice for my speedy recovery and each one brought good will and renewed us with hope. Their presence rekindled the love of God within me as I reflected joyfully on my private conversations I had with Sai Baba. I had learnt that suffering was indeed a divine calling card to strengthen us so that we learn to face pain, and with grace, are able to transcend it as Meera, in the Hindu scriptures, was able to do. She was known for her steadfast devotion to God and endured great pain without a single moment of sorrow.

Colleagues from the University of Hertfordshire, UK not only sent their good wishes for my recovery but also brought news about the success of my substantial grant application to the Government's National Institute for Health Research who had commissioned this work on depression in adolescents as a priority. Delighted that my hard work had been recognised, (for which I was nominated for the Dean's and the Vice Chancellor's Award) I looked forward to progressing this deserving initiative to help vulnerable young people.

I remember with great fondness the Liverpool Football Team's, motivating song "You'll never walk alone" which provided hope against all odds, ultimately winning by penalties heralding the Liverpool football team the European Cup Champions. This song, originally recorded by Frank Sinatra in 1945, is embedded in my heart reminding me never to lose hope against all adversities.

The Peruvian Paddington entered our home during this time, and we became the extended family of the Browns! As in the film, despite all the chaos he caused, he reignited the meaning of kindness and love and like the Brown family, our lives will never be the same again.

I am convinced of the presence of my inner guardian, a spirit that is ready to direct me to a new world beyond myself. My professional work had become the centre of my life for so long, and finally something happened, a paradigm shift in my consciousness in the way I now see my place in the world. People, places and activities became not only an integral part of my recovery, but also raised my levels of consciousness liberating me into new realms of purpose.

We do not define ourselves by what we do, what we have or what we feel, but rather by what we truly are. The footprints of the past leave an imprint, but we continue to walk forward in the present, in which we become free to dream to the rainbow's end.

Like a patchwork quilt, our lives can be stitched back even if the joins can be seen. Each piece is a memory that makes us complete. We are never alone for we are the waves in the vast ocean of benevolence. There are some people who are meant to be part of your journey, only to realise later the reason why they were there. And in our vulnerable moments we become spontaneously reconnected for our healing.

Rest and Recuperation

English Heritage Wrest Park

Come September I am here

NINETEEN

Life is a onetime offer

Life is not about waiting for the storms to pass; it's about learning to dance in the rain
– Vivian Green

What is absolutely certain is the uncertainty of life and rather than fearing it, I have learnt to accept it, without which we would not cherish the present moment. All the adversities that came my way made me stronger than before as I took charge of my life. Feelings of anger, frustration, hopelessness and guilt no longer ruled my life and I discovered love which shielded me from my own frailties. The setbacks that I endured became lessons in life to teach me about faith and hope. When I felt vulnerable, my tears irrigated my mind strengthening my resolve to reflect on precious moments. My mistakes became the tools I used to carve composure and my heartache sought the soothing balm of quiet pleasures. It was the cancer which taught me that I am not the cancer, but more than a cancer survivor reminding me that I am beautifully human and beautifully divine. Given a second chance, it's wonderful to fall in love with life again.

Embracing every part of me taught me to be kind to myself, thus releasing any ill feelings and ailments that were festering within me. Fears and anxieties steal the gift of time given to us by every breath for there is no promise of tomorrow. We as enlightened human beings need to be ever mindful of the fear of our old self-centred ways resurfacing having a detrimental effect on our well-being. From the moment of my diagnosis, there began a relentless period of 'Groundhog Day' where my predicament was not dissimilar to that of the protagonist Bill Murray, reliving the same events every single day. I chose to break free from the chains of habitual patterns of cerebral thinking which enabled me to transcend all negativity as I became more intuitive. This opened my heart to stay in faith, conquer fear, overcome all my limitations and have compassion towards myself and all others.

When Alice is riddled with questions, the Cheshire Cat enlightens her with the art of insightful living in the wonderland.

"Alice: Would you tell me, please, which way I ought to go from here? The Cheshire Cat: That depends a good deal on where you want to get to. Alice: I don't much care where. The Cheshire Cat: Then it doesn't much matter which way you go. Alice: ...So long as I get somewhere. The Cheshire Cat: Oh, you're sure to do that, if only you walk long enough." *(From Alice in wonderland, Lewis Carroll).*

It came to me some time later that the Cheshire Cat indeed had shamanic qualities! Our journey reveals everything that we need to know to be happy and contented.

My transformative journey is elucidatory, helping me to understand what is important and what isn't, and spending valuable time only doing what matters the most. Whether or not one has a good or a bad prognosis, my journey speaks of finding a meaning in all our

Alice and the Cheshire Cat by Daksha Trivedi

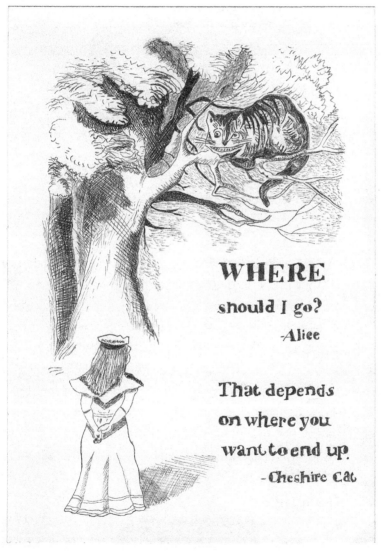

WHERE should I go? -Alice

That depends on where you want to end up. -Cheshire Cat

Tell me please

endeavours and sanctifying every moment. The onus remains with each person to find their true meaning of life as no one else can do it for them. Past events can become stepping stones for our survival, so therefore we need to learn the know-how of this process.

Innovative medical research continues to move forward in leaps and bounds. The recently awarded Nobel prize 2018 to James Allison and Tasuku Honjo for their discovery of cancer therapy by inhibition of negative immune regulation, established a landmark in the war against cancer. A large number of 'immune checkpoint therapy' trials are currently underway against most types of cancer, and we eagerly await the outcome from this new research.

Great strides are being made to detect early conditions that can increase a person's risk of developing oesophageal cancer. The Cytosponge is an innovative test pioneered by Professor Rebecca Fitzgerald at the University of Cambridge, that can be done in a GP surgery instead of a referral to hospital for an endoscopy for people with regular symptoms of heart burn, acid reflux or indigestion. It's a 'sponge on the string pill' that collects cells from the food pipe for detecting precancerous cells as early detection can improve patient outcomes. In addition, it is increasingly recognized that integrative or a 'whole person' medicine has a significant role in improving health and well-being[18]. To that end, it is important to consider the core principles of the Chopra Center's innovative and integrative approach to total well-being (https://chopra.com/mind-body-medical-group):

---

[18] Mills et al., J Altern Complement Med. 2016 Aug;22(8):627-34. doi: 10.1089/acm.2016.0002. Epub 2016 Jun 28.

- Health is not simply the absence of disease, but a state of higher awareness that opens us to greater wellbeing, creativity, and joy.
- The role of a doctor is to support people in restoring health and balance in their lives and to educate patients to make healing choices for themselves.
- The body and mind are inseparably connected. Both negative and positive thoughts, along with our deepest desires, create simultaneous physical reactions in the body.
- All of the healing traditions offer valuable tools, and the best treatment is one that uses the correct tool for the task at hand, including the practices of both conventional and complementary medicine.

They also suggest that practising gratitude takes us away from what is missing in our lives, awakens grace and makes our life complete[19]. Being grateful in the here and now creates new brain patterns which may even influence our gene expression in a more positive direction[20].

Acknowledging this hope for the future, I had reached a tipping point that forced me to escape from this prisoner's dilemma of facing the cancer journey alone. Living in the present, which is now, is not about hiding from what is coming. Ignoring the reality is the repudiation of our wakeup call. Within us, we all have the capacity,

---

[19] Mills et al., Spiritual Clin Pract (Wash D C). 2015 Mar;2(1):5-17.

[20] Summer Allen, Ph. D; The Science of Gratitude https://ggsc.berkeley.edu/images/uploads/GGSC-JTF_White_Paper-Gratitude-FINAL.pdf

the necessary tools and the presence of a benevolent spirit to guide us into the light where we rebuild ourselves.

None of us know when we will take our last breath. We breathe around 24, 000 times per day every day and still we do not consider how life sustaining this is. We know that doctors cannot keep patients alive by machines alone. After a while the patients have to breathe unassisted and their healing and recovery process is determined by this very force of life within them. I have learnt that every breath is mine and no one can breathe for me, nor can I for them. After my life changing event, I have no ordinary moments, for every second I live becomes extraordinary. I will spend the rest of my life making every breath count. Most importantly I understood the dictum 'Ask and it is given'. Placing implicit trust in the guidance from the higher consciousness, opportunities would present themselves to make the right thing happen at the right time by the right people. As Aristotle proclaimed, it is in our darkest moments that we must focus to see the light.

Almost a year on we returned to Madeira with our friends Rajiv and Priti, who had been so instrumental in preparing me to become fit for surgery. This time, it was a special celebration of my second life and being joyful to experience all the wonders of this world.

What a surprise on my birthday to hear Peter Knight, of my favourite folk band Steeleye Span from some forty-five years ago. He sang a special song for me at the Hitchin folk club from the 'Lullaby Kiss' that brought meaning to my whole experience:

This day is mine to keep until tomorrow
Its mine to live without rules to bind me
I could close every door so no one can find me
or I could open my heart and say Love come and blind me
The truth was no longer hidden in the words, it lived in my eyes
This life is mine, which I shall miss when it's time for the taking
which is why every day must be mine of the making.
One thing I know this life is mine

Celebrating life- Return to Madeira

I made it!

Amongst the birds of paradise

To my dear husband,
Without you, I would not be

When we gaze at the sky
We embrace its vastness
For I know your heart
Keeping us never apart

Your light that glows in all seasons
Healing this journey of ours
Beyond all our reasons

We stood the test of time
Your love infusing my soul
To the summit we climbed
Facing every blow

Autumn breeze softly brushes my face
You carry my spirit away
To our sacred space
Where together we stay

Time seems eternal as we stay awake
To the break of a new dawn
Then a rising sun awaits
To a promise of new life anon

Hand in hand with me
For what is all said and done
Without you I would not be

- Daksha Trivedi

TWENTY

Learning to talk about cancer

If we cannot do great things, we can do great things in a small way
Inspired by Napoleon Hill

My friend Nirmala and I used to speak regularly on the phone but this time it was different. I could sense from her voice that she was pained. I could imagine how visible this pain must be on her face, as she said that she had just received a gift she never wanted. I have heard this from many people and each time I tell them that all is not lost and hopeless, but I do understand why they would find it difficult to believe me. I thought about all those people who had allowed me to be part of their life and by my simply being there for them, we were able to create genuine bonds of empathy. In this closeness, they were able to release their damaging emotional burden.

When it happened to me, I felt alone not knowing with whom I could talk to and who would be prepared to listen. It wasn't a matter of fixing what was wrong, but more about being cared for and supported. In the rural area where I live, there is little, or no peer support and many people feel isolated unable to ask for help. Their diagnosis can be so overwhelming it diminishes their lust for life.

After several discussions with various cancer organisations, my husband and I decided to pilot a Macmillan supported cancer group in our village that would serve the needs of people who otherwise may not have anyone to turn to. We embarked on a programme of awareness to explore the feasibility of having such a group for both patients and their families, some of whom might be their sole carers. From the outset, enquiries began, and people dropped in with encouraging words of support.

At our first meeting, not knowing what to expect and with no preconceived notions, we were all able to talk freely and openly about ourselves, without any compulsion to do so. The common thread running through the group was the need to voice and express feelings. It was clear that beyond their treatment there was little or no support to deal with the emotional impact not only for themselves but also for their caring loved ones.

The support group became a network to connect with others who had undergone or were undergoing a similar or a different journey, where each person's unique experience had a profound impact on group members. Further monthly meetings identified the needs of individuals, what their expectations were and how we could mutually support each other to improve our well-being. Some people who were previously unable to talk were now able to express themselves without reservation, judgement or self-condemnation in this safe, trusted and compassionate environment. As the group grew in trust and confidence members began to open up and share their stories and experiences.

"My husband has been very low and negative, but for the first time we have come to a group that is about having a positive mind-set"

"I have been several years post-surgery, and I am not in remission, but remain cancer free. We are all going to die anyway, probably due to a completely different cause, but today I tell myself that I am well, and I do have a purpose to live. My box of positive affirmations is like a jigsaw puzzle, each one of you can have a piece. Together we can make a bigger picture of living well"

Spouses are often plagued with gulit that they did not do enough if their loved one did not survive. This feeling of inadequacy often remains with them for a very long time. A supportive group can provide reassurance that their loved one was cared for till the end, thereby reducing their heavy burden of guilt.

"I struggle with the thoughts of the cancer coming back. And I escape into becoming a workaholic…then the anxiety perpetuates." We discussed the practical and positive aspects of mindfulness-whatever we choose to do, meditation, affirmations, painting, nature walks and other activities that we enjoy are ways of dealing with fear so that it does not control us. The need to prioritise what is important and to achieve work life balance is an ongoing concern.

"I want to be in the group and not to pretend as if everything is normal. That doesn't mean I am re-living any experiences; it means I can let go and accept my new life"

"I am struggling as a carer for my husband whom I love very much. I am hoping that I will find the support I need in looking after him as his condition is deteriorating"

People also shared light-hearted anecdotes from their clinic visits and comparing notes would often result in fits of laughter accompanied by applause. In fact, a gentleman who used to smoke and drink heavily said he was grateful to his cancer for it changed his life and without which he would not be alive today! Thanking heavens for small mercies.

This group is evolving and exploring many facets of holistic approaches to wellbeing and to cherry pick what is most suitable for them. For example, side effects of chemotherapy have been of utmost concern and by sharing this brings relief to each and every one. They eagerly look forward to complimentary practitioners, health professionals and dieticians coming in to advise them on how best to manage food and their quality of life.

To my surprise, I met two other people who had also undergone an oesophagectomy, and we shared how we were dealing with complex challenges particularly around food, drink and pain management, even though we were aware that as individuals, we are likely to process foods differently. The common thread running amongst us was that consuming high energy sugar foods would trigger nausea and severe discomfort in our newly structured stomachs. In addition, without a food pipe we had to sleep elevated and this gave us the opportunity to find out more about aids that had been effective for sleeping. Others were able to contact support organisations for helping with physical and personal care.

Meeting each other face to face provides a visual perspective of how far we have come in our recovery, and this reflects the extent to which our strategies have worked. We also share what has not worked well, and together we are rolling stones of hopes and aspirations, recognising the vital role of using positive affirmations in our daily language. The environment creates self confidence and trust, with each person believing they are making a worthwhile difference in the lives of others.

'During my treatment, I believed that everyone would assume the worst about my diagnosis, which would give me little hope to focus on. For me, the most productive consultation was before surgery and I would have welcomed the discussions which took place then sooner' (D. Trivedi, excerpt from BMJ 2019)[21].

The pain I had felt for some time has now become my strength for all my tomorrows. Many great thinkers have recognised that people may often fail to remember our words or deeds but imprinted in their consciousness is how we make them feel. I am like a piece of art in progress which is continuously being shaped to help others find the love, care and support they desperately need and deserve.

Words matter when talking about cancer as many people use various metaphors. For me, the words 'fighting spirit and determination'

---

[21] Trivedi, D 'What your patient is thinking" Assuming the worst BMJ 2019;364:l788 doi: 10.1136/bmj.l788

drove me to active coping strategies. However, others would find this difficult depending on the stage of their cancer. We shared our views on some conflicting terminologies that influenced people's lives, such as 'Am I in remission or have I beaten cancer?"

We are learning to interact in a way that considers how we communicate the language of cancer. We are having to walk with 'a stone' in our shoe and every now and then we adjust it so we can continue walking. Even if the stone were removed, there seems to be a phantom presence.

Nearly two years after my initial diagnosis, I was able to bring up the subject of my cancer journey with some of my extended family. It came as a revelation to me that my cousin had an inkling that it could be cancer; we had mutually arrived at a juncture when we could broach the subject with a greater ease than ever before, especially as he saw my health greatly improved since his last visit. Talking about cancer will have its own time and place as it appears to me that the sufferer or their spouse or a loved one has to open the conversation. By doing so, we make them feel comfortable that it is fine to talk about it. Up until then, I felt that their natural curiosity might lead them to not only make a fatal connection but also assuming the worst outcome. We just need to handle our conversations with care and discretion when discussing sensitive matters especially gauging their readiness to engage in the dialogue. It may come as a surprise that on top of all the things we have to endure, it remains for us to break the wall of uncomfortable silence that keeps us from talking about cancer.

What to do?

For patients and families	For health care professionals
• Being aware of signs and symptoms and not to ignore them as early detection can improve outcomes, for example history of heartburn, acid reflux, etc whilst common may carry a risk of gastric cancer	• It is important to consider the background and cultural differences of all patients and their families, particularly older people, who may not understand and feel alone
• Talk to your health professionals about any family history of cancer and if unusual symptoms persist	• Consider the family history in a management plan as this may increase the worry and anxiety after a diagnosis
• Consult your clinical nurse specialist/oncology nurse for accessing ongoing support for example dietician and other appropriate care available	• Giving due consideration to how the facts and evidence around a diagnosis are communicated and understood so as to alleviate anxiety
• Macmillan services can identify local support groups and carers' organisations.	• Explore family and patients' concerns and give appropriate information, *particularly timely access to support*
• Complimentary/holistic approaches and self- management can improve overall well-being; seek appropriate professional/medical advice	• Making patients and their families aware of types of support for cancer including complimentary approaches, whilst not being prescriptive may be helpful
• Don't be afraid to ask and share for you may well get the required information and support that you desperately need but did not know how to access it.	*(Based on Trivedi, D. BMJ, 13 March 2019[15])*

Many visits to the Cross Cancer Institute in Edmonton, Canada with my brother where he received his treatment gave us a comforting experience of total care, in an exceptional facility with remarkable staff and volunteers. They were not just hospital personnel but they went beyond themselves like a 'family of carers' who contributed to our well-being in every way. In our most dire circumstances, they provided the much needed compassionate care. Whilst my brother was undergoing various tests and treatment, staff and young volunteers went out of their way to make us feel at ease. During this time we noticed some inspirational art called 'tiles' adorning the walls of the clinic with commentaries written by patients, volunteers and health professionals. We realised the extent to which they truly understood the feelings not only of patients but also their loved ones. It was refreshing to know that young volunteers also have a place in this care pathway and are greatly valued. These 'tiles' are a testament of the experiences of patients, their families, volunteers and health professionals whose dedication and commitment make a difference to the lives of many.

It's very difficult, at first, to come to grips with having cancer. However, after coming to terms with initial emotional upheaval, one reassesses one's priorities. Things that may have caused turmoil and stress recede and become minor. The pace we set ourselves to succeed, to accomplish, to "climb to the top", slows down considerably. We weed out the "non-issues" and come to appreciate again the important values of life, family, the beauty of life around us, and "being", rather than "having". The purity and infinite variety of our natural surroundings is the main theme of my tile. It is an expression of appreciation.

By a cancer patient, from the Cross-Cancer Institute,
Edmonton, Alberta, Canada

Water rings

One of the simplest past times for any age is skipping stones across water. If the stone is small and flat, and the throw is angled just right, the stone will skip across the surface of the water several times before it plops in.

Each time the stone touches the water, it creates a ring. Each ring moves outward in concentric circles. The first ring will mingle with the second ring. The second ring with the third and so on outward.

Cancer strikes one, then another, and another. It seldom has no effect. Thus, the water, or the pond represents life. The stone as it travels across represents cancer, the rings represent the effect upon others, and the ripples travel across the whole.

By a cancer patient, from the Cross-Cancer Institute,
Edmonton, Alberta, Canada

Having cancer is somewhat like peeling onions. Lots of tears at first, then going deeper, finding gifts, srengths and people, I never knew before.

Still there are times I just want the old innocent days back, when a long life and good health were taken for granted.

By a cancer patient, from the Cross-Cancer Institute,
Edmonton, Alberta, Canada

Butterflies are free. They emerge from a dark place and unfold their wings and fly. Their fragile beauty brings a light – heartedness to my soul. There is no noise or commotion, just a kiss as they light and float again. When I am burdened with tasks and worries and my heart is heavy, I try to remember butterflies. Like my patients they come on a whisper, come into my life, touch me gently and leave with a butterfly kiss. But I will not forget the beauty, the gentleness and the joy of feeling their presence and of knowing them a moment in time never forgotton.

By a health care professional, from the Cross-Cancer Institute,
Edmonton, Alberta, Canada

This tile is a rendition of my ideal design for a garden bird bath. Gardening is a past time I inherited from my mother. This was a great source of pleasure for her.

The quotation is borrowed from my father who is also a physician. " To harm never, to heal sometimes, to comfort always."

By a health care professional, from the Cross-Cancer Institute, Edmonton, Alberta, Canada

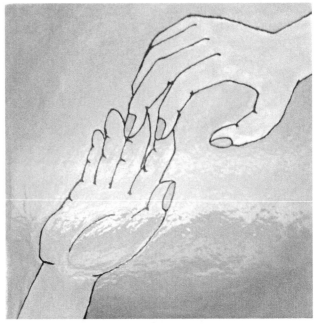

The healing hand

I have learned that volunteers help patients recover from their illness in a way that differs from physicians, nurses and other health professionals. In my tile, one hand represents the patient reaching out for someone to lift them up spiritually, emotionally , physically in any way he needs assistance. The other hand belongs to the volunteer who offers their hand to aid in the patient's struggle to regain their health. The warm colours in the background symbolise the volunteers' compassion and generosity bestowed on the patient; it also represents the sense of integrity and virtue a volunteer feels from offering their services. I have learned that volunteers are needed and appreciated by the patients and the volunteers have the capability to assist in the healing process. Volunteers have the pleasure of knowing that the "hand" they offer to the patients, helps them recover from their ailment.

By a student volunteer from the Cross-Cancer Institute,
Edmonton, Alberta, Canada

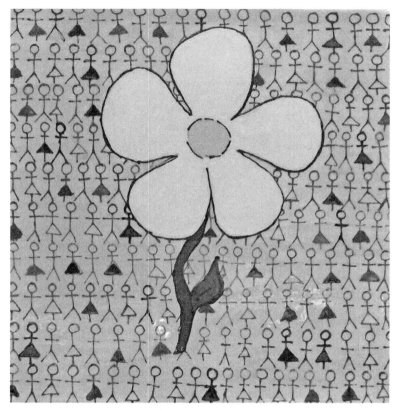

My tile reflects the experiences I have seen in people living with cancer. The people in the tile represent, the tremendous amount of support available to patients from family, friends and physicians. The flower represents a new level of understanding and personal growth in patients and those around them. There is an extreme strength felt when all these aspects come together.

By a volunteer from the Cross-Cancer Institute, Edmonton, Alberta, Canada

Life is like a sun flower

The full flower represents many stage in life. It represents fullness. The full petals bursting forth reaching to the warmth of "The Son" and beuaty we see in each day. The back petals are all the people who have influenced our lives. The light browns are the tint that has been engraved in me by my husband's love and support. The centre represents my children, surrounded by the petals of myself and my husband. When I have lived my life, I will fall away from my children leaving them to carry on. To mature, to become full ripe seeds to reproduce the beautiful flowers that will take our spot on this earth. The single bud represents new life. When examined closely, the bud will show a shade of yellow at it's time and within time it will become full new life in a beautiful sunflower. It will be nourished by the main stem from which we have been created.

By a patient from the Cross-Cancer Institute, Edmonton, Alberta, Canada

In God's Hand

I could not imagine going through this ordeal alone;

I surrendered myself into God's Hand.

I started to read books, listen to music, hear uplifting words, meditate and I learned.

I started to believe that everyone who prayed for me and sent me an abundance of positive energy was definitely a part of my recovery. I started to believe that we are all ONE in the universe, God being us and us being God.

I started to believe each of us is a God or Goddess in embryo and we therefore have to take responsibility by making the best choices we can every minute of our lives.

I started to be conscious of my choices.

I started to believe that we have to use our power of thinking as a tool to live our lives to the fullest.

I started to take responsibility when times were difficult and learned to say: "It's only a thought and a thought can be changed".

I started to believe that the more we give the more we receive and that for every inch of forgiveness we get a mile of peace.

I started to believe and I started to heal.

By a patient from the Cross-Cancer Institute, Edmonton, Alberta, Canada

Touched by lightening

This tile represents the magical moment of illumination and understanding people experience.

By a health care professional from the Cross-Cancer Institute,
Edmonton, Alberta, Canada

Not letting go

Many patients with cancer have taught me how precious today is. They have understood the challenge to us all "We have a choice: start dying now, or live until we die". One patient, who was also a nurse, helped me teach medical students even when she had advanced disease. She asked them to learn to listen so patients would not feel alone and would know the doctor cared. She was determined to live each day as much as she could; and she died watching TV with her children. My first patient was a very young woman. Despite attempts to help her with chemotherapy, she had widespread malignant disease and stubborn serious infection. Nearing death, rather than spend her time in hospital, she chose to spend her last weeks sitting on a beach, laughing with friends and listening to the waves and writing poetry. Both of these courageous women decided to live while they could. They refused to let go. Neither should we. And we can offer something better than chemotherapy or narcotic if we can say " Don't worry, I'm not letting go either".

By a health care professional from the Cross-Cancer Institute,
Edmonton, Alberta, Canada

"Each person's grief has its own
fingerprint.
Every journey of sorrow has a
unique map.
Hearts will heal on their own
timetable.
Never presume to know
how others should deal with their
pain"

John Mark Green

Epilogue

Since I received the devastating news of my cancer some two years ago, my life has taken a new turn. Having to live without an oesophagus, has brought many challenges, but thankfully this does not mean that I cannot enjoy my meals. In fact, I have expanded the range of culinary delights to such an extent that my family members now join me eating small portions more frequently. Though I do not have the sensation of feeling hungry due to damaged nerves, I have been fortunate to have retained the taste of food.

Walking daily along the now familiar country paths, I truly relish the exquisite sights and sounds of nature that fill my senses bringing wholesomeness to my life. Some days Badger would greet me with his familiar bark and the wagging tail and run to me with his lover's eyes, emanating such radiance that I rub my face on his inviting black and white furry coat.

My Caring Badger

Love in action

Dream field

I see potted plants reaching out exultantly to the sun against the black designed railings of our courtyard. I remember my mother feeding them with such loving care, just as she did me. Every day I see them blossom into new shades of colours like in a work of art. Learning to draw and paint is filling me with a meditative happiness where I feel close to my creator.

My vibrant soul feels elated with the music and movement of international folk dancing, as I float in ecstasy to the rhythms of the world.

In the garden of my heart

International folk dancing

My physical recovery continues in the gym and aqua circuits in the swimming pool, where I no longer feel so reticent about my huge scar on my right upper body. Jestingly I tell them that I have survived a shark bite! My first climb some eighteen months post surgery, to the summit of the mountainous area at the Geiranger fjord gave me a heightened sense of achievement. This is when I looked at the clear blue sky, against the sound of the thundering waterfalls nearby, and blew a kiss to the heavens above. My mother remarked that I was as strong as the mountain I had climbed that day. Later that evening, back on the cruise ship, I learnt the Latin American Bossa nova dance with my family joining in the gaiety of this special moment.

Every cancer patient's dilemma is "Will it come back?" It's almost like having the fear of heights, and it follows you like a shadow at every follow-up appointment. Walking down the same corridors and seeing other patients being wheeled to their scans, gives me flashbacks of my daunting experience. I reign in my fear with positive thoughts, reminding myself how far I have come not succumbing to a pessimistic outlook. Eighteen months on from my diagnosis, the consultant has conveyed to me that I have won the lottery, against all odds. My recent scans show some inflammation in my newly structured stomach tube but I thankfully remain cancer free.

Whilst maintaining work life balance, I have resumed my academic life with vigour leading a major project that gave me recognition in research excellence. I have also been nominated for the Research success of the year award in 2020 Vice-Chancellor's Awards. As a Senior Associate member, I am privileged to be part of the Bridge Initiative at Hughes Hall University of Cambridge, which aims to develop research translation into policy and practice for patient benefit. Upon invitation, I participated in the launch of this scheme in the presence of a member of the royal household, whose ingenuity opened up new horizons in healthy living initiatives.

Reiki healing practice continues to be an integral part of our lives and seeing its benefits on people is a reward in itself. Incorporating a mind, body spirit approach to health, I am continuing to bring balance and harmony in my life knowing that it is the body that heals and the mind gives it the space to do so[22].

---

[22] The Power of Your Subconscious Mind, by Joseph Murphy, Ph.D., D.D. Prentice Hall Press. 2011

It is my dearest wish to make time and volunteer once again on the Sathya Sai Mobile Hospital in India that provides doorstep medicine to the villages that have no other health care programmes. Internationally recognised[23] for its philosophy of transforming patients' lives through a holistic approach of *treating the patient and not just the disease,* this model of care has resulted in improved outcomes. Recognising the divine spirit in each person, the medical teams treat all with loving care. This model of care attracted medical electives not only from Cambridge but from other institutions, which provided a unique opportunity for me to be part of their training in delivering rural health and medical care. The experience fundamentally changed my perception about the multi-faceted doctor-patient relationship where physicians engaged with such empathy that both patients and their families benefited greatly.

---

[23] http://media.radiosai.org/journals/vol_12/01MAR14/Dr-Narasimhan-CNBC-TV-18-Healthcare-Award.htm

Health Care in Rural India

Director, Dr Narasimhan Sathya Sai mobile hospital
delivering health education

Where we serve

Health care practitioners in selfless service

I have re-connected with family and friends in a way that has healed broken wounds. In the storm, they became my stars, bringing a new spark of life. I relish my quiet communion with God, be it in service, prayer, healing meditation or in nature. I feel restored and my suffering and triumph speak only of gratitude and love. The greatest lesson is to accept pain and pleasure with equanimity, which puts you in good stead for the future. My testimony is an ode to my mother and my husband without whom I would not be celebrating this life.

We thank the Almighty for this second chance where our lives continue to be healed in every way. I am now living the dream to follow my purpose in this present, adding value and beauty to my life and others and living each day as if it were my last.

Fydor Dostoevsky alludes that "The mystery of human existence lies not in just staying alive, but in finding something to live for". Expanding my heart and mind and spreading my wings, I am discovering how much I can go beyond myself where no limits can bind me. Everything can be beautiful, not necessarily the way we want it to be. The passion in my new-found freedom lies in my ability to be eclectic, enjoying everything I do. I have understood that life is defined by not what we have given up, but what we have allowed in – strength, hope and empathy recognising frailty through kind heartedness and meaningful relationships.

I felt sad that I had so little time with my dear twin brother, and I wish we could have shared so much more. I treasured those ten months when we would speak on Skype often into the long hours until we met with him. Without so many words, he conveyed that our presence in his life at this time brought him solace and a sense of belonging. Cancer had brought us together putting an end to an acrimonious relationship.

One night we sat together and watched the film 'The Man Who Knew Infinity", a moving story of the great mathematician Srinivasa Ramanujan. We were entranced by this young man who described the rich colourful patterns of life and even though our lives are cut short, our dreams are eternal. We held hands every night in the inexplicable genuine moments of silent conversations, where unspoken words conveyed an understanding that found a place in our hearts. Though we were fraternal twins we were both together and separate at the same time. May we both meet some day somewhere in the celestial world where we will rejoice in a life well lived.

He left me with two gifts: a poem only days before he passed on and a fountain pen, not realising that this writing instrument would scribe the end of my story:

"No one comes to life with the knowledge of his or her lifespan.
We have no control over that. Only God has control over it.
When the Master of Time
Gently, serenely and divinely walks towards you
In order to see you through to the end of your time
The only prayer that should come to your heart is
Let there be at the least one thing that I did in my blessed time
that you can hold proud.
My Lord, for everything else, please forgive me".

- Deepak Dave, deceased 17 June 2017

The dawn of my new life welcomes me and fills me with boundless appreciation of all the lessons that steered me towards the path of love and forgiveness. I am now living with what Buddha calls the 'gladdened heart' where inner peace, joy and contentment are experienced. When circumstances change us, we must not see it as a loss but as an opportunity to realise all that we have. Though we are flawed, we are beautiful, sometimes damaged but also flourishing, and often frail but also invincible.

The reason for my survival is yet to be realised but what I am certain of is that I am discovering my true purpose in life. My cancer diagnosis was my appointment with God. Time is not like the tide for it moves only in one direction. When we leave this world, we must leave a treasure house of loving memories for those who walked with us. We will then have lived well and died well, and our hearts will be at peace.

"There are only two ways to live your life. One is as though nothing is a miracle. The other is as though everything is a miracle." - Author unknown

Together Again –
Daksha and Deepak

Till we meet again

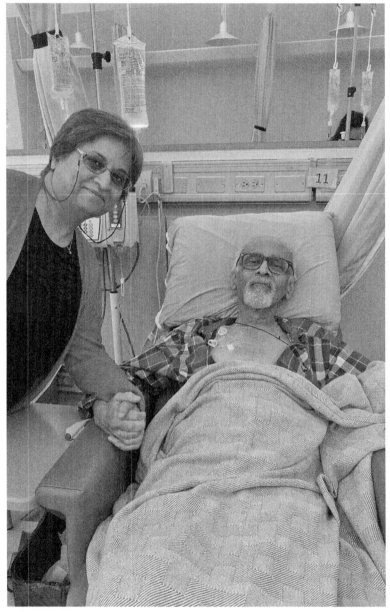

You are not alone

The way we were

Happy days

Look well to this day
for it is life
the very best of life.
In its brief course lie all
the realities and truths of existence:
the joy of growth
the splendor of action
the glory of power.
For yesterday is but a memory
And tomorrow is only a vision.
But today if well lived
makes every yesterday a memory of happiness
and every tomorrow a vision of hope.
Look well, therefore, to this day.

An ancient Sanskrit poem

I don't know how long I've got,
I'm just living the dream

Closing Remarks

by David Rennie, former Unificationist missionary to India and current Secretary of Interfaith Milton Keynes.

Dr Daksha Trivedi generously takes the reader together with her on a journey through what can be seen as a monumental struggle against a life-threatening bout with cancer which had already taken her twin brother. Her book describes the initial discovery, the diagnosis, the skilful operation and the eventual physical recovery and spiritual enlightenment that followed.

As a trained scientist in the medical field she was well aware of the physical consequences of such a disease, but as someone with a spiritual background, she was also aware of how the positive or negative attitude of a patient can influence the process of healing. Whilst healing is often perceived as a gift from the Divine, it is also the consequence of skilled treatment from brilliant doctors such as her consultant surgeon Mr Al-Bahrani.

In this book, science and spirituality are not seem as enemies, but as man's combined efforts to make sense of the world universe in which we live. When life challenges you and all certainties are shaken by the threat of imminent death, the quest for existential truth quickly intensifies. Reiki, Ayurveda and mindfulness sit quite comfortably with the paraphernalia of the Intensive Therapy Unit and the operating theatre!

The reader will never take life (in this world and even in the next) for granted after reading this book. Daksha has transformed her pain into her victory and as such has skilfully and subtly taught so many life-truths to the reader! The constant care and attendance of Daksha's loving mother and devoted husband throughout this engagingly written book often move the reader to tears and firmly instruct the reader in the holy values of family members who live their lives blessing others.

Throughout the book, gratitude shines out, to the doctors and staff of the hospital, to family and her circle of loyal friends, to her Guru Sathya Sai Baba, to God and to the beauty and fullness of life itself! I should conclude quoting her own words:

"We thank the Almighty for this second chance where our lives continue to be healed in every way. I am now living the dream to follow my purpose in this present, adding value and beauty to my life and others and living each day as if it were my last."

Daksha Trivedi was born and raised in Kenya and migrated to England with her family in the early 70's. She grew up in Coventry before pursuing her higher education in Liverpool, London and Cambridge. She now lives in Meppershall, a small hilltop village in Central Bedfordshire.

Daksha Trivedi trained as a scientist and obtained her Ph.D in studies of breast cancer (King's College, London); an M.Sc in the Faculty of Medicine, University of London and an M. Phil in Epidemiology at the Department of Public Health and Primary Care, University of Cambridge. As an academic, she has an interest in Evidence-based practice, public health and health care research.

She is an advocate of the patient forum of the Cancer Alliance Integrated Care Services Programme in the region to help promote early awareness of cancer detection and care services in the community. Her cancer journey has helped others and she now runs a local cancer support group in a rural area set up with the assistance of Macmillan Cancer Support. She conducts talks and workshops in diverse settings to help people access the support they need and to enable them to develop positive strategies. Daksha has a great interest in complimentary and holistic health programmes.

www.survivingcancer.co.uk

hello@survivingcancer.co.uk

Printed in Great Britain
by Amazon

60963727R00119